MW00936744

BEYOND SUCCESS

Redefining the Meaning of Prosperity

Jeff Gitterman *with* Andrew Appel

Balboa Press books may be ordered through booksellers or by contacting:

Balboa Press
A Division of Hay House
1663 Liberty Drive
Bloomington, IN 47403
www.balboapress.com
1 (877) 407-4847

Printed in the United States of America.

ISBN: 978-1-4525-9402-6 (sc)
ISBN: 978-1-4525-9404-0 (hc)
ISBN: 978-1-4525-9403-3 (e)

Library of Congress Control Number: 2014904567

Balboa Press rev. date: 08/07/2014

Contents

Acknowledgements

This book would not have been possible without the help and support of so many people, to all of whom we are very grateful. To Ellen Daly for helping to find the right words to convey, and to Julia Ferganchick Hilton for her help with editing and amazing typing skills. To the members of our families for their consistent love and support—Justin, Jake and Gianna Gitterman, Joelle Prisco and Zeva and Steve Appel, and to everyone at Gitterman Wealth Management for their loyalty and support, for they are the foundation upon which Beyond Success rests.

BEYOND SUCCESS

CHAPTER 1
Redefining Success

I dread success.
~ GEORGE BERNARD SHAW

Most classic success stories go something like this:

> *"I had nothing, but then discovered a new way of thinking, turned my life around and got everything I ever wanted…"*

I could tell you one such story. I went from debt and depression to having everything I ever wanted in the space of about two years. It all started back in 1997, when I was just another New Jersey insurance salesman, trying to support a wife and two small children on less than $20,000 a year, falling months behind with the mortgage payments, scared and unsure of my future. I was hiding my car at the end of every day because a finance company told me they were coming to repossess it. Debt collectors were constantly calling, and my wife at the time was close to a nervous breakdown. I had credit card debt, mortgage debt, car loans. Things looked pretty bleak. Then, one day…thanks to a life-changing conversation…I changed my way of thinking…and within only two years…but wait a minute. That's actually not what this book is about.

Yes, I turned it all around. I rose to the top of my profession and started my own wealth management company. I got the money, the house, the car—what I thought at the time was the life of my dreams—and in this book, I'll share some of the steps I took to get there. But before I do that, I want to jump ahead to the more important part of my story, which began once I got everything I thought I wanted, only to find that success wasn't what I thought it was. There was still something missing. I couldn't quite identify it, but I definitely didn't feel the way I thought I was supposed to feel, and when I took an honest look at my life, I realized that I was successful in all the ways I'd longed to be, but deeply, I still felt unfulfilled.

Now the word "fulfilled" can mean a lot of things to different people. The best way I can describe what it meant to me was that I thought I'd be at peace. I wasn't looking to retire, but I thought that internally I'd feel at rest. I'd been struggling to get something my whole life, and really did think that once I got it, I'd cross the finish line, reach the pot of gold—and the struggle would be over.

I'd grown up in a tiny apartment in Queens, NY, sharing a bedroom with my sister. My current income was more money than I ever could have imagined, and as the money came in I began buying more things and going on more vacations. Despite this, I still felt like I was chasing something. I had everything, but this insistent voice inside me kept saying, "This isn't it." I didn't know what else there was, and it slowly began to dawn on me that no matter how much money I made it would never make me feel that way I wanted to feel.

Of course, I'm not the first person to discover that having money doesn't necessarily guarantee happiness. These days there are countless books and research projects dedicated to the topic.

Most people who write about the "science" of happiness not only tell us that money won't make us happy, they also give all sorts of explanations as to why. It may have become a truism that money doesn't buy happiness, but when I look around at the consumer frenzy of our culture I can't help but feel that we haven't gotten the message yet. Decades of happiness research haven't seemed to have slowed down what economists call the hedonic treadmill, the seemingly insatiable pursuit of material things we think will bring us satisfaction.

I think a treadmill is a good analogy. I've also heard it described as a hamster wheel or an eddy at the side of a stream. These images suggest that we seem to be stuck in a trap or closed loop when it comes to the pursuit of success and happiness, but knowing that the loop doesn't work doesn't seem to be enough to get us out of it. In order to free ourselves from the trap, perhaps we not only need to take a look at the results of our efforts, but also at the underlying drives and convictions that make up the loop itself. If we keep doing the same thing and it doesn't produce the results we want, it must be because of certain unquestioned assumptions and motives that keep sweeping us back around into this stagnant eddy. Many of us live out our whole lives this way, because we haven't stopped to question these things.

The intention of this book is to help create a meaningful definition of success, attain that success, and most importantly, enjoy that success. In order to do that, let's start by taking a closer look at some of the fundamental issues. Let's talk about money, let's talk about happiness, let's talk about desire, and then let's talk about what success really means.

Putting Money Back in its Place

Let's start with money. I'm a financial advisor, so it's a subject that's certainly close to my heart. I often like to open my seminars and talks by asking people to give me definitions of what money means to them, and I usually get a similar range of replies: *freedom ... security ... opportunity ... power.* I've asked this question to hundreds of financial advisors over the years, and I rarely hear the standard dictionary definition, which is that money is simply *a means of exchange.*

I define money as a means to satisfy a desire. That may sound like a straightforward definition, but where things get complicated are when we start to measure our satisfaction, happiness, and success by how much money we have. Money is then no longer simply a means, but an end unto itself, trapping us in the loop. Through the work I do, I see proof on a regular basis that having a million dollars in the bank has no relationship to happiness—but people continue to insist that it does, even when their experience shows them otherwise. Many of my clients who have reached this milestone tell me they still wake up in the morning and feel the same way they felt when they were broke.

I've also witnessed another interesting occurrence with many of the people I work with. Often, if a client's net worth is hovering around, say, the million dollar mark—the markets, being what they are, tend to play games with this important milestone in their life. They can look at the numbers and see that one day they have just over a million, but the next day it's dipped back down into the high six figure range. In reality, these fluctuations have absolutely no impact on our daily existence, and yet many people freak out when they see the numbers dip. They're measuring their happiness by a financial marker to such a degree that it has a huge impact on their day-to-day emotions.

The philosopher Arthur Schopenhauer once wrote, "Money is human happiness in the abstract; and so the man who is no longer capable of enjoying such happiness in the concrete, sets his whole heart on money."[1] Through my work, I meet far too many people who are living their lives in this abstract realm: they have material success, but they are unable to really enjoy any of it.

I also have something of a unique vantage point in my work, because my client base includes a large number of college professors—men and women with not only an unusual degree of financial stability, but also a good deal of job security and free time. Yet even among this demographic, I see degrees of happiness and fulfillment that vary extraordinarily.

To be clear, I'm not arguing against the importance of money—as Woody Allen put it in his inimitable manner, it's "better than poverty, if only for financial reasons."[2] That's a funny quote, but it makes a very important point. It puts money in its place. Money itself is a neutral force. It's not good or evil, moral or immoral. Some people love to quote the Bible as saying that money is "the root of all evil," but I think it would be more accurate to say that "*attachment to money* is the root of all evil." That makes a lot more sense. After all, money is a *currency,* and the source of the word currency, or current, means *a condition of flowing.* If money gets clogged up with meanings and desires that we've assigned to it, whether it's blocked out of our lives or hoarded in our bank accounts, then it is little wonder it becomes unhealthy, like a stagnant pool cut off from the current of a river.

Forget About Happiness

Implicit in the statement "money won't buy us happiness" is the idea that something else will, even if we don't quite know what that something is. Most of us, when it comes down to it, are searching for that elusive something, whether it's money, love, power, work, spiritual knowledge, or something else. What do we mean when we say "happiness?" Usually, it represents a certain emotional state—a feeling of peace, joy, or satisfaction that we may have experienced in brief moments of our lives and that we want to experience as much as possible. That's what I spent the first few decades of my life looking for, until I discovered that money couldn't buy me that feeling.

Think about how hard it is to sustain any particular feeling for more than a few minutes—or perhaps a few hours at most. The next time you feel happy, try it—see how long you can hold onto that feeling before something triggers a negative emotion and happiness slips from your grasp. Our emotional experience fluctuates constantly, and is based on any number of factors: internal and external, rational and irrational, objective and subjective, biological, psychological, environmental, chemical... the list could go on and on. If we stop and think for a moment about the confluence of circumstances, both inner and outer, that we'd have to control on a permanent basis in order to remain perpetually happy, we can quickly see that this level of control is impossible.

Even if we isolated ourselves in a beautiful place, surrounded with everything we could ever need, our hormones could still trigger emotional states over which we have no control. Our emotional experience is not something we can control all the time, and yet most people in our culture believe that the ultimate goal is to be perpetually happy. If that's how we define success, we're setting ourselves up for failure.

Desire and the Brain

Our definition of happiness is often what gets us caught in the trap of wanting more of what we can't seem to get. As we've all experienced, when we get the things we want, they usually don't live up to our expectations, at least for very long. We then set our sights on a newer, bigger, better, more beautiful, faster object of desire and feel that sense of anticipation again, convincing ourselves that that this will finally be the thing that satisfies us once and for all.

Scientists can even explain the physiology of why this happens. Financial writer Jason Zweig, in his entertaining and insightful book *Your Money and Your Brain,* describes going to a neuroscience lab at Stanford to participate in an experiment where he was put inside a scanner that traced his brain activity while he played an investing video game. What the study showed was that in the moments when Zweig anticipated a big win, the neurons in a certain part of his brain went wild. In contrast, whenever he actually won some money, the response measured by the scanner was far less intense. What this revealed, as tested on Zweig and many others, is that the human brain is wired to experience more pleasure in the anticipation of a reward than in actually getting it. Modern science was able to prove, as Danish philosopher Soren Kierkegaard observed almost two centuries earlier, that "the fulfillment is always in the wish."[3]

I see this all the time with my children. They use up so much of their energy wanting something they think will make them happy: a cell phone, pair of designer sneakers, video game, etc., but once they get it, they suddenly don't seem so interested, and before long, they're wanting something else.

I won't try to explain the complex physiology of what some scientists call the "seeking system" here, although I would recommend *Your Money and Your Brain* for anyone interested. The point that's relevant, and that has been backed up by numerous studies is that, as Zweig puts it, "The pleasure you *expect* tends to be more intense than the pleasure you *experience*."[4] There are perhaps evolutionary reasons for this, but as Zweig concludes,

> …the seeking system in our own brains functions partly as a blessing and partly as a curse. Our anticipation circuitry forces us to pay close attention to the possibility of coming rewards, but it also leads us to expect that the future will feel better than it actually does once it arrives. That's why it's so hard for us to learn that the old saying is true: Money doesn't buy happiness. After all, it forever feels as if it *should*.[5]

Breaking Out of the Loop

If nature did in fact design us this way, how are we to break free? Spiritual teachers from numerous cultures and religions have offered answers to this question for centuries—ways to liberate ourselves from what contemporary Buddhists sometimes call the "wanting mind." The Buddha saw *tanha*, the blind craving for objects or sensual pleasures, as the root of all suffering. Numbers two and three of Buddhism's Four Noble Truths state that "Suffering arises from attachment to desires" and "Suffering ceases when attachment to desire ceases."[6]

Buddhist teachings guide spiritual aspirants to find liberation from *samsara,* which contemporary Tibetan Buddhist teacher Sakyong Mipham defines as "a wheel that is endlessly spinning...a circle of illusion that keeps us ending up just where we started."[7] Such schools of wisdom, both Eastern and Western, as well as more contemporary spiritual teachers like bestselling author Eckhart Tolle, teach us to dwell in the present rather than live in constant anticipation of the future. They can all show us powerful techniques for living in "the now," and enable us to taste moments of freedom from the endless craving of the mind.

The problem, however, with many of these approaches is that if we're not careful, these moments of freedom and bliss can simply become new objects of desire that we hope to experience all the time. Before we know it, we're back in the loop, chasing a temporary feeling in the hopes of making it permanent. While success cannot be defined solely through money and the material things we have, neither can it be defined solely by the internal things we feel.

Ironically, we often judge our own success by how we're feeling, but we usually don't apply the same standard to others. When we think about someone we admire greatly, who we would say lived a successful life, does it matter to us how they felt? What do we really know about the inner experience of Martin

Luther King Jr., Nelson Mandela, or Mahatma Gandhi? For the most part, we tend to measure their success by the tremendous impact they had on the world. Do we think Mother Teresa was less successful in her mission because we now know, thanks to the publication of her journals, that she was plagued by doubt and desperation, or do we simply look at how many lives she saved and perhaps even feel a greater admiration knowing that she did it despite how she felt?

Beyond Success

In order to create a meaningful definition of success, I believe we need to find a different way to measure it other than by what we have or how we feel. When I got to a point in my own life where I found myself successful by common standards but far from happy, I had to rethink what success was all about. For the past several years I'd been chasing a dream, visualizing my goals and attaining them one by one—and I found a lot of joy in that process. I didn't know then that my brain was wired this way, but I later saw from my own experience that there was more joy in chasing the dream than there was in actually getting it.

It wasn't so much that I was unhappy with the results of my success. There was nothing wrong with having the money, and it sure was nice not to have to worry about paying the bills each month, but I had attained everything I wanted and was missing the thrill that came from the pursuit itself. Now, we could conclude from this experience, as many brain scientists do, that our evolutionary wiring is a kind of curse, condemning us to perpetual let-down. The anticipation mechanism can seem like a cruel trick of nature. But I looked at it another way. I realized the problem wasn't that the goals I'd reached weren't good enough—the problem was that I was standing still again. I had no journey anymore. I then understood that I needed a journey, a direction, a dream, and I started to turn my attention to the journey itself, to a sense of striving and reaching ever-higher, and sought my happiness there, rather than in any particular outcome. I guess it's a kind of living in the moment, but it's a moment that's always moving.

When we begin to understand that there is nothing we can get that will ultimately make us happy, we can stop striving to endlessly accumulate—and when we begin to pay less attention to how we feel as a way of measuring our success, we will find that we have a tremendous amount of energy and attention at our disposal to give to others and to ourselves. We can then redirect our "seeking system," and enlist it towards what we want to express in the world, rather than what we want to get or how we want to feel. This is what I discovered when I set out to find what lies *beyond* success, and to redefine success itself in the process. That's what this book is about: my *beyond success* story—and hopefully yours too.

I say *beyond success* because success is not an end point, a state of outer wealth or inner peace that we can achieve and then stop growing and evolving. We, as human beings, are not made to stop. We are creatures of change, curiosity, and creativity who need to have our goals set a little *beyond* our reach. In the chapters that follow, I'll explore several ideas, distilled over the years from my own life experience and from those I've had the pleasure of knowing and learning from. I'll then offer four pillars on which to build a *beyond success* story. It is my deepest hope that this path can take you, as it has taken me, beyond the things we thought would make us happy.

CHAPTER 2
A New Currency

Tell me to what you pay attention and
I will tell you who you are.
~ JOSE ORTEGA Y GASSET

The model of success I want to share in this book doesn't use money as its primary currency. If we're to create a new model of success that isn't measured by how much money we make or how we feel moment-to-moment, we will need a new means to that end. Money, as we've been discussing, is merely representative, and creates a lot of problems when we use it as a measure of our success. Therefore, we need to begin by identifying a new standard of measurement.

The word *currency* originally meant a "condition of flowing," and was only given its common meaning, "circulation of money" in 1699 by British philosopher John Locke. The terms that we associate with money—flow and circulation—are very appropriate. Money is not something we can create, but we can encourage or block its flow into or out of our lives.

Traditionally, money has been assigned four characteristics, which old-fashioned economic textbooks had a rhyme for: "Money is a matter of functions four: a medium, a measure, a standard, a store." These days, the functions of money tend to be described as a medium of exchange, a unit of account, and a store of value. I would add one more to these, one that we may not find in economic books, but that is perhaps more relevant to success than any of the standard definitions, which is that money carries with it the flow of *energy*. However tangible it may seem, money is actually an abstract representation of something intangible that has far more substance than the paper it's printed on. When I say energy, I don't mean a physical sensation of feeling energetic as opposed to tired or lethargic—I mean the life force we bring to everything we engage in—be it a personal interaction, creative collaboration, physical challenge, or mental puzzle.

Growing up, I had an intuitive understanding that everything in the world was a movement of energy. I didn't buy the story that kept showing up in front of me that said the world was only made up of people, places, and things. I saw the world as energy, and I actually saw that the only thing that was really important was the joint flow between human beings and how that energy was working and processing.

This understanding is something that has been known to spiritual mystics for quite some time. Over the past 30 years, we've increasingly seen a greater synthesis of Eastern and Western ideas than ever before, and during this same time period, Western science has begun to validate many of the key insights of Eastern and Western spirituality. I love this quote from Max Planck, a German physicist and contemporary of Einstein who won a Nobel Prize for his research with atoms, and who is considered by many to be the father of quantum theory:

> As a man who has devoted his whole life to the most clear headed science, to the study of matter, I can tell you as a result of my research about atoms this much: There is

> no matter as such. All matter originates and exists only by virtue of a force which brings the particle of an atom to vibration and holds this most minute solar system of the atom together. We must assume behind this force the existence of a conscious and intelligent mind. This mind is the matrix of all matter.[1]

Here is a scientist basically telling us that the fundamental element of reality is not matter, but energy. Other quantum physicists will tell us the same thing, often in rather mind-twisting statements, but these ideas are not just esoteric territory of the scientific fringe. In 1632, Galileo published *A Dialogue Concerning Two Chief World Systems*, which included his principle of relativity, which states that the fundamental laws of physics are universal in all fixed situations. Others such as Isaac Newton and Albert Einstein continued to build on the work of Galileo, which eventually led to the discovery of Einstein's famous Theory of Relativity in 1905. $E=mc^2$ states that energy equals mass times the speed of light squared, and that energy and mass are transmutable.

More recently, scientists such as Stephen Hawking have been looking to take the work of Einstein further to find a complete set of laws on how the universe works, in what has become known as Unified Field Theory. Although this has yet to be conclusively proven, it's hoped that in time it will be found and eventually simplified so that it can someday be taught in schools, thereby giving everyone some idea of how the Universe operates.

This is obviously a very brief summary of a much deeper and complex subject, and there are certainly numerous books and other resources available on this topic for anyone that would like to understand it in more detail. For our purposes though, I hope we can simply agree that at the most basic level, energy is what we exchange with each other and the world in every action and interaction we have.

Let's take a look at some practical examples. Most of us have heard that speech itself accounts for only a small percentage of the actual way we communicate. If this is so, what makes up the rest of that communication? Energy. When I was a child, I used to find it hilarious that I could look at a dog and say in an angry tone of voice "You're a good dog!" and then watch his shoulders and tail slump over as if he were being yelled at. Then I'd turn around and say in a really loving voice, "You're a bad dog!" and would crack up as he'd jump around and start wagging his tail as if he was being praised.

It's the same with human relationships. How often do we come across someone who says one thing to us, but by the vibe we're picking up, we know they mean something quite different? Most people can probably say they've had the experience of saying "hello" to someone they don't like with a nice big smile on their face, when all the while both people know they don't like one another. This probably happens in business more often then we'd like to admit. The "hello" and the smile don't really change a thing, because it's not in the words. It's the energy behind the words.

Sometimes, when I'm speaking to business people, they'll agree with this basic premise—that energy is the basis of everything—but complain that they find the concept of "energy" too vague or ungraspable. So I ask them, besides money, what is the currency through which we exchange our energy?

Where Attention Goes, Energy Flows

Attention is often defined as a concentration of the mind or a close or careful observing or listening, but these definitions do little to evoke the power of this intangible force—economically, politically, socially, personally, or otherwise. Although attention may seem too intangible to be considered a currency or a commodity, think about the ways we use the word. We talk about *paying* attention. We *need* attention. Someone popular is the *center* of attention; someone needy is always trying to *get* our attention. As intangible as it may seem, our attention is the currency of countless transactions we engage in every day.

Why is attention so powerful? Because what we choose to put our attention on is where we direct our energy, in all its many forms, including our time, creativity and of course, our money. More simply put, *where attention goes, energy flows.*

Let's take a metaphor from the natural world. The earth receives its fundamental source of energy from the sun and plants have sophisticated systems to capture and convert that energy. While sunlight in its natural form is a source of warmth, it doesn't have much power *per se* because it's spread out in so many directions, but when sunlight is focused and concentrated through a magnifying glass, it suddenly becomes far more powerful. When harnessed in this way, the power of sunlight can start a fire, and when the power of light is condensed to a much greater degree it can become a laser that cuts through steel.

In the same way, our mind, with its power of attention, acts as a focusing agent—a magnifying glass through which our energy can be amplified in its impact. If we train our attention, it too can become like a laser, a powerful tool for cutting through many of the illusions and misconceptions that keep us trapped in the loop I described earlier.

If you're still not convinced that attention is a commodity, let's look at how the major players in the business world relate to it. Corporations today spend thousands of dollars researching where our attention goes as we surf the Internet, and thousands more creating sophisticated strategies to capture that attention. It's no accident we talk about *paying* attention.

If you've seen the movie *Minority Report,* you may remember the scene where Tom Cruise's character walks into the mall, passes through a retina-scanning identification device, and is immediately besieged by personally tailored ads addressing him by name, anticipating his every desire. That may have seemed like science fiction when the movie came out only a few years ago, but these days something surprisingly similar happens every time we go online. Software can now track which sites we visit on the Internet, where we click, and how long we stay on a page—in other words, what catches our attention—in order to present us with future ads that match our interests. Advertisers not only want to know what we're looking at when we go online, they also want to know which corners of the screen we look at first and how many seconds we spend there. This is why certain parts of a web page are more expensive to advertise on than others.

Information Overload

Can you begin to appreciate why our attention is so valuable? I believe it is fast becoming one of the most valuable commodities of our time, and yet we are so very far from being in control of it. There are so many things vying for our attention that we've lost, in many if not most cases, the ability to control where it goes. Indeed, our attention can seem to have a mind of its own, and our information-saturated lifestyles are in many respects making this situation worse.

"A wealth of information creates a poverty of attention," wrote pioneering economist Herbert Simon, in a remarkably prescient 1971 article.[2] With more and more corporations, politicians, entertainers, charities, and salesmen of all kinds competing for our focus, it's no wonder we often feel as if our attention is scattered or fragmented.

Recent studies show that those of us who've grown up watching television have actually been unconsciously trained to track rapid movements of information, which is why we find watching TV numbing and soothing. These days, many channels on our TV screens often carry one, two, or three additional messages in the space around the picture we're watching, and when it comes to the Internet, there can be countless attention-grabbers on a single page, not to mention the pop-ups. Our kids often need even more stimuli and sometimes watch TV or play video games while also sending text messages or listening to their iPods. According to the National Institute of Mental Health, between three and five percent of children (approximately 2 million in the United States) suffer from Attention Deficit Hyperactivity Disorder (ADHD).[3]

When we think about it, all this clamoring for our attention seems like it would be exhausting, but have you ever noticed that it's a lot easier to watch television than it is to do something like meditate? That's because our attention is so accustomed to being drawn outwards, pulled here and there by a multitude of competing objects, that the simple act of sitting still and doing nothing has become difficult if not nearly impossible.

Back in the fifties, there was an outcry when market researcher James McDonald Vicary came up with the concept of "subliminal advertising" and declared that he was sending moviegoers hidden messages telling them to eat popcorn and drink soda. The whole thing was later found to be a hoax, but it hit a nerve. We feel vulnerable to things like subliminal advertising and brainwashing because deep down we know we're not really in control of our attention.

Our attention is in fact a commodity—a source of value that's being solicited constantly—and a currency that we are conducting business with every day, whether we are conscious and in control of it or not. It is also the currency of our most personal relationships, and it is often in these areas that we find ourselves the most impoverished.

Let's take an example. Have you ever gotten to the end of the day feeling overwhelmed, out of control, and exhausted, even though you've barely left your desk? At times like this, have you felt like you don't have the energy to go home to your family? In these moments, don't you just long for someone to listen to you?

For most of the busy professionals that I work with, this scenario is all too common. However, what many people don't consider is that the experience of being overwhelmed isn't just a result of all the external pressures we deal with every day. Whether in the workplace, at home, or walking down the street, we're bombarded with so many competing demands—pulled this way and that by email, phone calls, billboards, window displays, and people knocking at our doors—it's no wonder we've lost control of our attention.

An Essential Part of Life

If you have children of your own, or have spent much time with the children of friends, you probably know that kids crave attention. In fact, many kids want attention so much that they don't care if it's positive or negative. If a child discovers that the only way to get attention from their parents is to misbehave, they will do so even if the desired attention comes in the form of a punishment. The need for attention will outweigh the fear of the punishment that comes with it.

A very powerful testament to this can be found in politician John McCain's autobiography *Faith of My Fathers*. McCain was a fighter pilot in Vietnam and spent about five and a half years in captivity as a POW. He writes of being held in solitary confinement:

> It's an awful thing, solitary. It crushes your spirit and weakens your resistance more effectively than any other form of mistreatment. Having no one else to rely on, to share confidences with, to seek counsel from, you begin to doubt your judgment and your courage. But you eventually adjust...as you can to almost any hardship, by devising various methods to keep your mind off your troubles and greedily grasping any opportunity for

> human contact...The punishment for communicating could be severe, and a few POW's, having been caught and beaten for their efforts, had their spirits broken as their bodies were battered. Terrified of a return trip to the punishment room, they would lie still in their cells when their comrades tried to tap them on the wall. [But] very few would remain uncommunicative for long. To suffer all this alone was less tolerable than torture.[4]

Our desire for attention is a big part of what makes us human and comes from our longing for interconnectedness with each other. When all else is stripped away, as in the extreme circumstances McCain describes, being able to connect with other human beings can even be what keeps us alive.

The Real Energy Crisis

How we direct our attention is very important, as it determines where we will *spend* our energy. In a world where attention has become a primary currency, we can begin to better understand our values by looking at what we give our attention to. This may seem like a simple concept, but it's amazing what problems can be created if we're not conscious of how this works. Since attention goes where energy flows, it's essential to become conscious of our spending habits.

Let's look at some of the ways we unconsciously spend our attention and how we can begin to regain control of it. When we're feeling depleted, where do we usually look to refuel? More often than not, we look to other people. When we feel drained or overwhelmed, we usually look for someone else to give us their attention, hoping it will make us feel better. In our attention deprived society, what are we really craving? *Energy*. This is the real energy crisis at hand.

When we want someone's attention, we really want their energy. This is why someone who is always playing the victim, demanding us to listen to their shopping list of woes, drains us. It's also why someone who is selfless and giving of their attention lifts our spirits when we're around them, leaving us feeling invigorated and refreshed.

There's nothing wrong with exchanging energy with others, as that is clearly what relationships are about. In our interactions with other people, we're always in a dance of energy. What directs the flow of that energy and choreographs the dance is our attention. All this being said, when we recklessly spend our attention and energy on meaningless distractions and then look to each other to get it back, we can see that we will quickly create an unsustainable situation. It's like all of us going out with our credit cards and spending thousands of dollars on things we don't need, and then coming to each other and borrowing money to buy food and pay the rent. Sooner or later, we're all going to go bankrupt.

Think about all the different people we come into contact with during a day and how these different interactions make us feel. Some people we know may demand a lot of our attention; others may give freely of theirs. Relationships are all based on an exchange of energy that is sometimes agreed upon and often times not.

It's interesting to consider that we're very conscious about how physical activity uses up energy, but we're not so conscious about how mental attention uses up energy. We would never spend all day jumping from one place to another without stopping to rest and catch our breath. Yet we let our attention be constantly pulled from one object to the next, and whether we know it or not, our energy goes with it.

Have you ever watched a small puppy when it's just been let out into a yard? It will run all around, crossing its own path, following its nose from one scent to another. If you trace its path you are most likely left with a meaningless, directionless scribble. As long as we're not the masters of our attention, we are like that puppy.

Moving Towards Wholeness

Generally speaking, there are three places our attention wanders. The first, as we've been discussing, is outward toward all the things in the world that distract us. The second consumer of our attention is our ego, which we can usually recognize as the voice in our head that never seems to stop talking. It's the voice that often says we're not good enough or that we don't yet have all the things we deserve. This voice is often the trigger that causes us to venture outward again and again to try and find the one thing we think will satisfy us once and for all. Whether it's the right job title, an ideal relationship or enough money—we're out to prove to that voice that we're OK.

Although we all most likely feel quite alone with this voice in our head, I think it is comforting to know that it is one of the things we all share in common. The people we see in the world who radiate success have simply learned how to channel this voice into an energy that pushes them towards their creative purpose, which is the third direction our attention can go—toward creative expression and toward others. We will explore how to cultivate this later in this book, but the first step is simply to notice how much of our attention is spent listening to the incessant inner voice in our heads and searching outward for something that we hope will quiet it.

The good news is that we can regain control over our attention and begin to harness its extraordinary power in such a way that will create much more energy for us, and also leave us with plenty to give to those who really need it. Once again, where attention goes, energy flows. This, in many ways, is why what is known as "the law of attraction" holds true. The basic idea behind the law of attraction is that what we think about is what we attract; what we put our attention on is what we manifest. There's certainly a lot of truth to this principle, although its workings are perhaps a little more subtle than the common New Age translation: "think positive thoughts and you can have anything you want."

My understanding of the law of attraction is not about using our thoughts to miraculously conjure up what we think will make us happy—as that won't work for all the reasons we discussed in the last chapter. There are many books out there that tell us all we need to do is put our mind on something and it can be ours. The problem is that even if we do this and get what we think we want, we're still caught on the hamster wheel I described earlier.

The people who truly radiate success are filled with a clear sense of life purpose and their attention is constantly focused on that vision. That becomes their reality. By giving our attention to our own creative purpose in the world, we become a vehicle for generating more energy than we can imagine.

Take some time to think about attention in some of the ways I've shared in this chapter. Become familiar with this new currency, and begin to reflect on your own "spending habits." Throughout the book, I'll be referring to attention as the currency for going *beyond success.* I'll show you how to take control of your attention and then use your newfound power source to change your life, achieve your deepest dreams, and if you choose, begin to transform the world around you. My approach to success is about turning our attention around and realizing that we have an incredibly powerful resource that, when used correctly, cannot only transform our lives but also those around us.

CHAPTER 3
A Core Investment Strategy

If one is not willing to invest psychic energy in the internal reality of consciousness, and instead squanders it in chasing external rewards, one loses mastery of one's life, and ends up becoming a puppet of circumstances.
~ MIHALY CSIKSZENTMIHALYI[1]

As a financial advisor, my job is to make maps. People come to me from all walks of life, each with their own unique set of financial circumstances, ideas about money, spending habits, needs, and dreams, but they all come because they want to get from point A to point B. Point A could be anything from a quagmire of debt, a comfortable stipend, or a multi-million dollar inheritance, but point B is always the same: happiness. So my job, at least in theory, is to help my clients take control of their relationship to money, and in the process create a map that leads them towards where they wish to go.

Now, for all the reasons we've discussed, this doesn't always work so well in practice. Not only will money most likely not make us happy, but our ideas about happiness are probably based on some questionable conclusions about how we'd like to feel all the time. I'm not trying to knock my own profession, as taking control of our financial lives is a very important step towards finding our peace of mind and sense of direction. However, the currency of happiness is less tangible than dollars and cents. Time and again, I've seen clients who've gotten their finances in order but still lack a deeper sense of fulfillment, and I can often see that they are still recklessly spending far more precious commodities; namely their energy and attention.

Another way I think about my job is that I'm kind of a financial doctor. People call in a financial advisor because they know their relationship to money is unhealthy. They don't necessarily know the causes, but they're suffering from the symptoms, and they want me to give them a diagnosis and a cure. What I've discovered over the years is that if I'm going to help them heal their relationship to money, I have to help them heal their relationship to their mind and how they see the world in general. As I learned about the power of attention and started to transform many aspects of my own life, including my relationship to money, I began to look at how I could help my clients save, earn, spend, and invest the most valuable internal commodities they own.

I sometimes think of my work as "Wealth Management for the Soul," and this book as an "Investment Plan for Our Attention." There are four pillars to this plan, and each of them can be correlated to a key component of financial wisdom. These financial correlates, however, are not just metaphors, as I don't believe it's possible to have a healthy relationship to money without first having a healthy relationship to our attention. So these four pillars are not only foundational for financial success, but they can also bring us many of the things that money can't buy. I've discovered in my own experience, and in that of many people with whom I've worked, that following these principles can lead us to a happy destination—but it probably won't look or feel like we expect it to!

My Four Pillars of Success are:

Connecting to Source
Owning Our Unique Expression
Redirecting Our Attention
Expanding Our Awareness

You may notice that the first four letters of each pillar spell out "CORE." I like this acronym, because it connects back to my investing metaphor. Financial advisors often refer to the central part of a client's portfolio as their "core holding." The core requires investments that will be reliable year in and year out. They need to be strong and steady. Having a strong core holding allows us to be creative and take risks with the outer edges of our portfolio without losing our financial balance. Investing our energy and attention in the way these pillars describe is what gives us a core holding as a human being—a sense of stability, integrity, wholeness, and purpose that provides a platform for our creativity to flower.

Another reason I like the acronym "CORE" is that it points to the idea of core strength. Have you ever been told by a trainer or physical therapist that you needed to develop your core? That's why we all do sit ups, Pilates and exercises on large inflatable balls at the gym. The idea is that rather than training isolated muscles like an individual bicep, we work to strengthen the muscles that support everything we do to keep us stable and balanced, particularly those in our abdominal area and back. It's a more holistic approach to strength training and one that builds a foundation for continued development.

Many people I meet tell me they feel out of balance and scattered, and I think a lot of this stems from the fact that we tend to treat the different areas of our life like isolated muscles—our business lives are separate from our spiritual lives, our personal lives are separate from our financial lives, etc. We check our spiritual values at the door when we enter the office and then wonder why we feel like we are two different people at home and at work.

These four pillars are about building core strength, not at the physical level, but at the invisible level of self. Just like a financial plan, the basic principles of the four pillars are always the same, but they're infinitely customizable to each individual's unique needs and circumstances. They're principles and practices directed at the core muscles of our self-sense, and if we work them out on a regular basis, they can provide us with stability, balance, and coordination, so that we are then able to do far more than we could imagine possible.

Core Investment

The first pillar, **Connecting to Source**, focuses on how to become more aware of our attention, and then how to save and spend it wisely. Through the practice of meditation, we can break the illusory promise that something "out there" will give us the energy we crave, and instead teach ourselves to connect to an infinite Source of energy that exists within each of us.

The second pillar, **Owning Our Unique Expression**, focuses on how we earn our energy. Rather than seeking energy from outside of ourselves, we can learn how to discover and enact our *unique creative expression* in the world—meaning what we sense we are truly here to do with our lives. Discovering our true purpose in life can fulfill us more than any amount of money or any object we can possess, because it continues to generate energy as we engage in it. Each of us has something unique and special to offer the world, and this pillar can help us discover and own our true purpose while also making money in the process.

The third pillar, **Redirecting Our Attention**, is about how we invest our energy, and shows us how to direct our attention towards who we want to be in the future. I often tell my clients that if they don't invest anything for retirement it's not going to be much fun when they get there. In the same way, if we don't invest our attention in the future, but rather let it constantly dwell on the past or pursue short-term desires in the present, we will unlikely be able to create the kind of future we truly want.

The fourth pillar, **Expanding Our Awareness**, is about how we give our energy to others. Many people come to a financial advisor not only to get their finances in order, but also because they have a desire to use their money to help benefit the world. Many people actually find that this is what ultimately gives them a sense of true purpose and meaning. In the same way, when we regain control of our attention, we will find that we have something of tremendous value to give back to others, thereby enriching our own lives and those around us in the process.

So let's get started on our journey. In the chapters that follow, I'll explain how to build core strength and invest it wisely so that our success not only becomes a source of personal fulfillment, but also an overflowing wealth of energy and creativity that we can share with the world around us.

~ The First Pillar ~

Connecting to Source

Each one has to find his peace from within. And peace to be real must be unaffected by outside circumstances.
~ *MAHATMA GANDHI*

CHAPTER 4
Saving and Spending in an Attention Economy

The energy of the mind is the essence of life.
~ ARISTOTLE

One of the first pieces of advice I usually give my financial clients is to put a portion of their income into a savings account before they do anything else with their paycheck. Ideally, I suggest they take ten percent of what they earn and put it away, and then they can pay their bills, go shopping, or do whatever else they'd usually do.

The first pillar is very much about doing the same thing with our energy. Throughout our lives, we all waste money to varying degrees, and unfortunately most of us do the same thing with our attention. If we don't find a way to connect to our energy and generate reserves within ourselves, we'll most likely find that we don't have enough to get us through the day.

The good news is that there is a Source of power and energy in the Universe that we can all plug into—it's just that most of us have not really been taught how to do it. Yet we've all tasted it, at least at times. We've all had moments where our minds were rendered quiet, perhaps while watching a beautiful sunset, witnessing the birth of a child, or staring into our lover's eyes. These moments give us strength, energy, and power that usually come from someplace deep within.

If you look around the room you're sitting in right now, you will most likely see a power outlet in one of the walls. Unless you're an electrician, you probably don't know what happens behind that wall, but you know that if you plug something into the outlet it's going to work. The same can be said for each of us, although we rarely seem to know where to find and how to plug into the Source of our internal energy and power.

We've all experienced moments of inspiration where we suddenly find access to a far greater surplus of energy and discover capacities we didn't know we had. In moments like this, we are connecting to Source. A musician playing in front of an audience, a scientist pursuing a medical breakthrough, an athlete "in the zone," or an aid worker saving lives are all examples of how people plug into Source in different ways, although the examples need not be so extreme. Each of us channels this same Source in our own unique way and in varying degrees throughout our lives.

People around the world have different names for this Source, and if you'd prefer to call it God, Love, Spirit, Chi, or anything else that feels comfortable for you, that of course is fine. I use the term Source because it takes away a lot of the strongly charged beliefs that tend to get associated with such an idea. It helps keep things simple, and this way we can hopefully find that we agree far more than we disagree. For the purposes of this book, I'd like to leave aside all our different beliefs about what Source looks like, and see if we can simply agree that there is a Source—and if this Source is the essence of everything—it is one thing that we all have in common beyond our belief systems, racial differences, and cultural value structures.

Plugging Into Our Power

If everything is energy at the deepest level, then the more tuned in we are to the Source of energy in the Universe, the more we can actually accomplish. Any truly successful person understands this to some extent. The simplest way to understand the first pillar is that it has to do with finding a way to plug in on a daily basis to access our power.

As we've begun discussing, many spiritual traditions consider the thinking, wanting mind to be one of, if not the greatest obstacle to better understanding the world as it truly is. Mental conditioning, evaluations, and judgments are seen as mechanisms that prevent us from fully connecting to the larger energetic system that surrounds us. This may be even truer in this day and age; when all of us are bombarded with so many distractions it's no wonder we can't keep still. As we've all experienced, the voice in our head is often talking so fast that at times we can barely concentrate on anything. I was recently walking in New York City next to a homeless man who was talking to himself aloud. As crazy as this sight so often seems to us, it dawned on me that most of us are doing the exact same thing, just silently to ourselves rather than out loud.

Sometimes I ask people in my seminars to give me an image that describes their mind. A six-lane highway is a common description. An endless to-do list is another. Other images people come up with include an orchestra without a conductor, a jigsaw puzzle with only some pieces joined together, or a traffic jam at a busy intersection. Almost without exception, people come up with images that represent chaos, confusion, fragmentation, complexity, and lack of integration.

Generally speaking, there are two ways our mind works. If we have a project, task, or problem to solve, we can engage it to help us accomplish our goals. When we use our mind in this way, it is working for us.

The other way our mind works is when it endlessly chatters and we don't seem to be able to control it at all. It's just running amok, depleting our energy, and not really accomplishing anything. For much of the day, most of us are not engaging our mind, but rather our mind is engaging us, and during these times there probably isn't much it's telling us that's particularly useful. It's just trying to keep us hooked—on it. As the saying goes, "the mind is a terrible master but a wonderful servant."

Regaining Control

One of the simplest ways to describe the first pillar is that it's an opportunity to reclaim our power over our mind, so that rather than it holding us captive for most of the day, we can become masters of our attention. The more we are able to quiet our mind and allow space for whatever lies beyond our "wall," the easier it will be for us to tap into our power, and the more Source will be able to fuel us. The first step in learning how to harness our attention is to become aware of how it moves, and in order to do this we need to find a way to disengage from the continual stream of thoughts that preoccupy us. This is one of the fundamental reasons people practice meditation in all of its many forms.

When I use the term meditation, I don't necessarily mean sitting cross-legged on a cushion, but rather participating in any deliberate activity that teaches us to disengage from a compulsive relationship to our stream of thoughts. Although some type of traditional sitting meditation is probably the most direct and effective way to do this, there are many other techniques, and each of us should find a method that seems best for us. For some it will be a meditation cushion. For others, it might be a walk in nature, a long bike ride, or perhaps a kickboxing class. What we do is not nearly as important as how and why.

You can even try meditating right now as you're reading this book. If you pull your attention away from the words on the page for a minute and watch the thoughts that are going through your mind, they might go something like this: *I have to go to the bathroom … the ball game is on … my mother-in-law is coming tomorrow … I have to go to the dry cleaners before six … that food smells good …*

If we start to observe our thoughts, we will begin to see that they are just fragments, and each one of these fragmented thoughts can be a hook to bring us into a larger, longer, and more drawn out story—that can then easily string together into paragraphs, chapters, and books. *That food smells good …* could perhaps lead to *I wonder what's cooking. Gee, my wife is a great cook; I wonder if she's also making that broccoli soufflé I love … I'm so hungry … but I really shouldn't eat that anyway because I'm supposed to be on a diet. I can't believe I've gained so much weight recently. I really should sign up for the gym again and start going regularly. Otherwise how am I ever going to fit into that suit for my sister's wedding?* On and on it goes.

If you've ever tried to meditate, you've probably discovered that gaining control of your attention is much easier said than done. I once read a Zen parable where a monk was asked for the secret to enlightenment. The monk replied that he could guarantee enlightenment to anyone who can give him their full attention for twenty-four hours. You can probably guess how many newly enlightened people there were the next day.

I'm not going to ask you to try the same thing, but let's try a simpler exercise. Close your eyes if you'd like, or if you prefer, look at the blank page next to this one, and try not to think one thought for one minute. Not one.

What you probably found if you tried this exercise is that you can't stop thinking for a couple of seconds, let alone one minute. If you feel so inclined, try this exercise again for twenty seconds and see how you do. The important thing is to be really honest with yourself. How long can you go without thinking a thought? To perhaps make things a little easier, try focusing on your breath and count each time you inhale and exhale. See if you can get to twenty without thinking about anything else. Most people who do this, especially for the first time, find that they'll get distracted and lose focus before they reach the count of five or ten.

Although all of this may seem depressing at first, reclaiming control of our attention is a very learnable skill, and once learned, we will be able to direct our energy more effectively in ways that we want. The power of a practice like meditation is that we get to see how our mind works and how often it makes us do things we'd perhaps be better off not doing. In the usual course of a day, when we grab hold of a random thought and begin turning it into a longer story, those stories often lead to action. Before we know it, *I'm hungry* becomes a bag of chips or a cookie. *My mother in law is coming tomorrow* becomes a fight with your spouse over their mother's overly frequent visits.

A lot of people who begin learning how to meditate erroneously think that the ultimate goal is to stop thinking all together. This is a big reason many people give up in the early stages, because as you probably experienced in the last exercise, *it is impossible to stop thinking.* If we begin to learn how to meditate thinking we're going to train our mind to stop, we're going to feel let down and frustrated very quickly. The objective is to discover that although we can't get rid of our thoughts, we can let go of our *attachment* to them. We can let our thoughts continue down the six-lane highway of our mind at a hundred miles per hour and simply not take them seriously at all.

The Means is the End

Connecting to Source is not about any one specific practice, and it's not a means to an end—it's an end unto itself. Most of us are so used to having a goal in everything we do: making money, getting a promotion, finding a romantic partner, etc. With meditation, there is no end point, which is also why some people find it so challenging. In our fast-paced modern world, many of us seem convinced that unless we're constantly running on the gerbil wheel trying to keep up, we're not going to accomplish anything and may even get left behind. Ironically, even paradoxically, thinking this way wastes a tremendous amount of energy and further depletes us.

Have you ever seen someone at the gym who runs from one machine to the next doing exercises very quickly, and then wonders why week after week they have no results? Compare them to someone else who has an incredible physique and does slow, concentrated exercises that really work the muscles. Who's better off in the long run?

Just as we go to the gym to maintain a healthy body, we can meditate to maintain a healthy mind. The first few times we go to the gym, it's really difficult and we're sore afterwards, but the more we go the better our body is able to perform. We become stronger and usually have more energy during the day. With meditation, the more we practice, the more access we gain to the stillness and power that lies beyond our racing thoughts.

I see the benefits of meditation clearly when I look at my own life. If I think back many years ago, I can see that although I focused on successfully growing my business, I did so at the expense of my family, friends, and myself. In the years since then, as I've begun to train my mind through meditation, I have much more energy to accomplish things. In the last decade, I've grown my company to ten times the size of what it was while spending more time with my family and friends. Although I have a lot going on, most people tell me I'm calmer today than I've ever been. I have plenty of quiet time, and also time for social events. Without question, I would attribute this directly to meditation.

The benefit of learning how to disengage from our thought stream is that we can then apply our minds toward more constructive activities. Meditation creates an opening and a deeper space within, which then allows for more energy to flow through us. In this seemingly paradoxical way, increasing the space and stillness in our mind allows us to accomplish more in the world.

The important thing, as we will see, is to learn to spend at least five, ten, or perhaps even fifteen minutes a day, every day, meditating and working with our attention in a way that is comfortable for us. This will help us tap into a greater Source of energy that can carry us through the rest of our day—helping us to be more present, focused, and available—which in turn will help to bring more creativity, success, and happiness into our lives.

CHAPTER 5
Pathways to Silence

Through meditation one realizes the unbounded. That which is unbounded is happy. There is no happiness in the small.
~ THE UPANISHADS[1]

If we can make Connecting to Source a daily practice, and ideally something we do first thing in the morning, we will begin to see a more natural flow to our lives and feel less reactive towards the world. If you've never meditated before, or have tried it a couple of times but not done it consistently, this chapter will offer you a variety of ways to develop a practice that will hopefully work for you.

If you already have a meditation practice, engage in daily prayer, or have some personal way you like to connect to a deeper sense of silence and stillness, that's great, and you are of course welcome to apply any of the principles of this book to the practice you're already doing. At the same time, perhaps take a moment to think about whether your practice feels alive and powerful, or whether it's reached a plateau. If it has, perhaps consider making a few changes or trying something different to see if it helps you break through to a new level. Remember, what we do is not nearly as important as how and why. What matters is that we take some time each day—and it may just be a few minutes to begin with—where we consciously watch the thoughts that race through our mind and actively practice detaching from them.

Ways of Meditating

This chapter contains some of the best examples of meditation techniques I've found. You're welcome to adapt them in whatever ways work for you, or create your own scenarios, as long as they serve the function of releasing attachment to thought. I'll also share a few of my favorite meditation metaphors and use them to illustrate some of the benefits of these practices as well as a few of the challenges they can present.

There are many meditation techniques that can be used in a variety of ways, and it's my hope that the instructions and visualizations in this chapter can be of help to you, regardless of whether you are just starting out or have been meditating for a while. There are many great books that have been written on the subject, a few of which I will mention, and of course nothing beats a live teacher or meditation class if you feel like you need help getting started.

Sitting Position

It's important that we sit in a position that we can maintain without moving for the duration of our meditation time. Please don't try sitting in a full lotus position if you're not an accomplished yoga practitioner—you'll find that after a couple of minutes your legs will be in pain—and you'll most likely have a hard time dealing with the flood of thoughts racing through your mind about it. If you like, you can try sitting on a firm cushion with your legs loosely crossed and your back straight, or if it's easier for you, feel free sit on a chair with your feet touching the floor. The most important thing is that we are still, alert, and not distracted by physical discomfort.

Focusing on the Breath

Once we've found a comfortable sitting position, the next step is to turn our attention towards how we are breathing. I recently learned that the word *spiritual* originates from the Latin *spiritualis,* which means *breath.* The process of breathing, which we often don't give a second thought to, is the most basic expression of life, and so it seems fitting that many forms of spiritual practice are based on observing the flow of breath.

Try this: *Breathe in.* If you're like most people, your chest probably expanded and your stomach sucked itself in. That's what most of us do when we're instructed to take a breath. We tend to take only shallow breaths that fill out our chests, but we rarely breathe deep into our bellies, which is what the human body is designed to do. Our stomach should go out when we take a breath in. Concentrate on filling up your stomach when you breathe so that it expands, and then let it contract as you exhale. I recommend practicing this for a few minutes before you try any of the other exercises in this chapter. Vietnamese Zen master Thich Nhat Hanh gives the following instructions:

> Your breath should be light, even, and flowing, like a thin stream of water running through the sand. Your breath should be very quiet, so quiet that a person sitting next to you cannot hear it. Your breathing should flow gracefully, like a river, like a water snake crossing the water, and not

like a chain of rugged mountains or the gallop of a horse. To master our breath is to be in control of our bodies and minds. Each time we find ourselves dispersed and find it difficult to gain control of ourselves by different means, the method of watching the breath should always be used.

The instant you sit down to meditate, begin watching your breath. At first breathe normally, gradually letting your breathing slow down until it is quiet, even, and the lengths of the breaths fairly long. From the moment you sit down to the moment your breathing has become deep and silent, be conscious of everything that is happening in yourself. [2]

Be Gentle with Yourself

Meditation in its most successful form is a very gentle process, and if we encounter difficulties, it's very important that we not judge ourselves. In the beginning, we may find ourselves drifting in many directions and we may quickly become frustrated. It's important that we be gentle with ourselves, especially during these times.

I actually find this to be one of the most challenging parts of the practice. As soon as I lose my focus, my mind will further derail and say something like, *Ugh, pay attention! Focus, focus, focus! I'm a terrible meditator!* When something like this happens, try to remember that these are just additional thoughts that may seem attractive to cling to because we're so used to judging ourselves. Like the rest of the thoughts we've been talking about, simply let them go as gently as you can.

When we start learning to meditate, an analogy that is often used is that of a baby learning to walk. In the process, a baby may fall down many times, but he or she doesn't say, "What's the matter with me? I'm such a crappy walker!" Babies don't judge the process at all. They simply keep trying to walk, and are willing to fall down as many times as needed until they learn. If we can take this attitude with us as we start to meditate, we'll find that we can progress much faster. We should again remind ourselves frequently that there is no goal to reach. We are simply and gently cultivating a state in which we are able to watch our thoughts without attaching ourselves to them. Tibetan teacher Sakyong Mipham describes this experience as "placement." In *Turning the Mind into an Ally,* he writes:

> Each time you choose to recognize and acknowledge a thought and return your consciousness to the breath, you are learning placement. It's such a small act, so innocuous, but it's one of the most courageous things you can do. When you recognize and release that thought, you can take pride in yourself. You've overcome laziness. You've remembered the instructions. You can feel happy coming back to the breath. Don't worry that you're going to have to do it again—you're going to do it thousands of times. That's why it is called practice.[3]

Other Points of Focus

Other traditional aids to meditation include the use of a short phrase, prayer, or *mantra* which we can use to help focus our concentration. In many Eastern traditions, the most basic mantra is *Om* or *Aum,* representing the indivisible One reality. You can also choose a traditional phrase if you like, such as the Tibetan *Om mani padme hum.* According to the Dalai Lama, this mantra promises that by practicing a path of skillful activity and wisdom, we can transform our impure body, speech, and mind into the pure exalted body, speech, and mind of a Buddha.[4]

Some schools of Christianity espouse the practice of contemplative or "breath" prayer. Best-selling author and pastor Rick Warren advises readers of *The Purpose-Driven Life* to "choose a brief sentence or a simple phrase that can be repeated to Jesus in one breath: 'You are with me.' 'I receive your grace.'...You can also use a short phrase of Scripture."[5] Judaism, Islam and all other world religions and spiritual traditions also have powerful meditative phrases and prayers, or you can create your own, such as "Love," "Peace," or "Harmony." I recommend finding something that has personal meaning for you.

The Stream Meditation

One of my favorite ways of meditating is what I call the stream meditation. Start by picturing yourself sitting in a paradise garden. Imagine that it's a beautiful day, with a warm breeze and the scent of spring in the air. It's completely silent, except for the sound of a stream flowing in front of you. Sit down cross-legged on the grassy bank, right by the water's edge. Take a deep breath, all the way down into your stomach, and slowly exhale. When a thought arises in your mind, imagine that it's a stick, log, or tangle of branches that you then simply drop into the stream and let float by.

If you're a beginner, you may find that during this meditation you can let go of one thought, and perhaps another, but by the time the third or fourth pops into your head, you start following one of those thought-sentences until soon you've created a whole story. It's like jumping into the stream and grabbing hold of one of the logs. One minute we're sitting on the bank watching every thought go by, but before we know it we've been carried away. If that happens, simply climb out of the water, return your attention to sitting by the side of the stream, and once again practice watching your thoughts pass by.

Train of Thought

Another way of meditating that a lot of people find useful is the train meditation. I sometimes add my own variations, but this metaphor comes from Steven Levine, who wrote *A Gradual Awakening,* one of the best books in my opinion for beginning meditators. This technique led to some of my biggest breakthroughs in understanding how my thoughts were creating my emotional states, and these realizations were key to helping me gain more control over my attention:

> An image about practicing meditation that may be helpful is that of standing at a railroad crossing, watching a freight train passing by. In each transparent boxcar, there is a thought. We try to look straight ahead into the present, but our attachments draw our attention into the contents of the passing boxcars: we identify with the various thoughts. As we attend to the train, we notice

> there's supper in one boxcar, but we just ate, so we're not pulled by that one. The laundry list is the next one, so we reflect for a moment on the blue towel hanging on the line to dry, but we wake up quite quickly to the present once again, as the next boxcar has someone in it meditating and we recall what we're doing. A few more boxcars go by with thoughts clearly recognized as thoughts. But, in the next one is a snarling lion chasing someone who looks like us. We stay with that one until it's way down the line to see if it got us. We identify with that one because it "means" something to us. We have an attachment to it. Then we notice we've missed all the other boxcars streaming by in the meantime and we let go of our fascination for the lion and bring our attention straight ahead into the present once again.[6]

A Mind Like the Sky

Here is another meditation I like from American Buddhist teacher Jack Kornfield. In an article for *Shambhala Sun* magazine titled, "A Mind Like the Sky: Wise Attention, Open Awareness," he offers instructions for practicing an "opening" approach to the mind:

> Sense that your mind is expanding to be like the sky—open, clear, vast like space...As you rest in this open awareness, notice how thoughts and images also arise and vanish like sounds. Let the thoughts and images come and go without struggle or resistance...Problems, possibilities, joys and sorrows come and go like clouds in the clear sky of mind.[7]

Walking Meditation

Some people find sitting still on a cushion uncomfortable, and others find it unbearable for a variety of reasons. If so, you might want to try a form of walking meditation. When practiced sincerely in a quiet place, a walking meditation can be just as powerful as sitting and may be easier to incorporate into our daily lives. It can also potentially allow us to be more aware of our body.

Just as with any sitting practice, it's important to set aside a specific time for a walking meditation, even if it is only a few minutes each day. Don't try to combine it with running errands or exercise, rather give your full attention to the practice. I like to walk and meditate outdoors, although a quiet indoor space can also be a good venue as long as you're not disturbing others. You can even use your living room if it seems suitable.

Before you start walking, focus on your breath in the same way that you would to begin a sitting meditation. Let your awareness follow your breath, in and out, helping you to calm and focus before you begin walking. Once you're ready to begin, start walking slowly, keeping your movements gentle and relaxed, and let the rhythm of alternating between the right foot and the left foot help you settle into a meditative state. Try to keep your eyes down or let your vision blur a little so that you don't become distracted by anything in your visual field. If you find your attention getting caught by your surroundings, simply bring it back to the rhythm of walking and breathing.

The basic idea with a walking meditation is that the physical experience of walking becomes an object of focus in the same way that our breath or a candle flame might be in a sitting practice. As you walk, pay attention to the sensations in your body. Notice how walking is not just something we only do with our legs, but something we actually do with our whole body. If you find it helpful, you can start by focusing on the soles of your feet and then slowly move your attention up through your entire body. Release any areas of tension, and if at any time you get caught up in your thought stream, simply bring your attention back to the act of walking.

Common Obstacles

There are many reasons people get stuck, derailed, or discouraged when meditating. Here are a few common ones to watch out for:

> MIND COMBAT. It's not a good idea to let ourselves get into a battle with our mind, because it thrives on energy. If we resist it, we actually feed and give it energy. So try to avoid meeting your mind with resistance. Rather than sitting down to meditate with the idea that you're going to conquer your mind, just sit and let it be. We will find over time that our mind calms down by itself if we don't fuel it with resistance.

> THINKING WE DON'T HAVE TIME. A lot of people think they don't have time for meditation, but when we begin to appreciate its value and realize how much it liberates our attention and creativity, we will hopefully begin to understand how important taking time to meditate can be.

DEALING WITH OLD WOUNDS OR SCARS. Meditation can be a cleansing experience, but the process can sometimes bring old psychological and emotional wounds to the surface that we may find difficult to face. While actually meditating, it's probably best to not get caught up in trying to directly deal with these issues, but rather let them go like any other thought. However, we may find that in conjunction with our meditation practice, we might want to spend some time with a therapist who can help us to heal any wounds that may arise.

SPIRITUAL PRIDE. Some people feel a sense of spiritual power from meditating, especially once they become very good at it. This is also something to be avoided! Meditation is about our own personal relationship with Source; it's not something we should ever use to feel superior to others.

EXPERIENCE ADDICTION. If we take the practice of meditation seriously, sooner or later we will probably experience moments of deep peace and bliss, but we need to be careful not to attach ourselves to these experiences either. Many people try to create deeper meaning out of such occurrences and lose their meditative awareness in the process. The most common problem with good experiences is that once we have one, we either want to hang on to it forever or have another one as soon as possible. Our meditation practice can then potentially become another form of craving—a kind of spiritual consumerism or addiction to higher states of consciousness. Don't look for or cling to the highs. Instead, seek steadiness and consistency. Remember, the purpose of meditation is to let go of our attachment to all thoughts—and that means everything.

GOAL FIXATION. For those who've been meditating for years and are hoping to eventually find a permanent state of bliss, it's important to remember that the point of meditation is not to rest in light, clarity, and peace forever. It's a constantly unfolding process, and as long as we are doing it earnestly, we'll keep hitting new and deeper layers. If we're open to the process, it will enrich our lives greatly.

Remember, meditation is a practice, which means we have to stick with it to see the benefits. When we practice regularly, meditation can help to ground and focus our attention in ways that few, if any other endeavors can. It may take discipline to set aside five, ten, or fifteen minutes every morning, but it will pay off. Meditating regularly can help us save energy for when we really need it, and will also help us spend our attention more wisely throughout our day.

~ The Second Pillar ~

Owning Our Unique Expression

If a man is called to be a street sweeper, he should sweep streets even as Michelangelo painted, or Beethoven composed music or Shakespeare wrote poetry. He should sweep streets so well that all the hosts of heaven and earth will pause to say, here lived a great street sweeper who did his job well.
~ *MARTIN LUTHER KING, JR.*

CHAPTER 6
Earning Energy

Everything—a horse, a vine—is created for some duty...For what task, then, were you yourself created? A man's true delight is to do the things he was made for.
~ MARCUS AURELIUS[1]

A hundred years ago, it would have been pretty easy to tell a person's income level and social status at a glance. All we'd have to do was look at the quality of the clothes they were wearing, the other luxuries they had, and the way they traveled. Today, much of that has changed. As a financial advisor, I know better than most that a person's lifestyle can bear little or no relationship to their income.

I've shown up many times for meetings with new clients—parked next to their sports cars and admired their beautiful homes—but when I delved into their financials, saw that their income was nowhere near what they need to fund the lifestyle they're living. It's then no surprise when they tell me they're maxed out on credit, double-mortgaging their homes, and not saving anywhere near enough for retirement. They are classic examples of what we call living beyond our means.

However, I work with other clients who live in more modest homes and drive less expensive cars, but also have a substantial amount of money saved for retirement. By living comfortably within their means, these clients are usually much more satisfied with their lives and experience greater peace and joy.

Unfortunately, in our consumer-driven culture, living beyond one's means has become a very widespread and acceptable practice for people of all ages. Young adults are now often overspending before they're even out of school, using their student loans to buy things like designer clothes or fancy mobile phones without thinking twice about it. According to the College Board, during the 1990s, the average student-loan debt doubled, and by 2004 the average college graduate was starting his working life with a debt of $17,600.[2] Many people I know don't pay off their student loans until they are well into their thirties.

One of the most basic pieces of advice that any good financial advisor will give is that we can't afford to live beyond our means. This seems like an obvious point when it comes to money, but in many ways it's just as true when we apply it to the currency of attention and the energy it carries with it.

We all engage in certain activities that drain our energy and others that increase it. Another way to say this is that certain activities require an expenditure of energy while others seem to earn it. It's not true that all restful activities give us energy, or that all stressful and demanding ones deplete us. Even sitting at a desk all day can leave us feeling drained depending on what we're doing, and there are things many of us love to do that are physically, mentally, and emotionally challenging, but leave us feeling energized and rejuvenated. It might even be an activity that's very demanding and stressful, like working in an emergency room or building a business, but the key is that the activity itself gives us fulfillment.

The second pillar, Owning Our Unique Expression, helps us identify the activities and modes of expression that earn us the greatest amount of energy. Once we've done this, we can then begin to align our lives and work with those larger sources of energy income. When I say unique expression, I don't necessarily mean having a special talent. We don't have to be a concert pianist, Olympic athlete, or the person who finds a cure for cancer. Our unique expression can be found as a plumber, teacher, hair stylist, CEO, stay at home parent, engineer, or banker, just to name a few examples. It can be any activity or job where we find our joy and sense of purpose in life. Simply put, our unique creative expression is the thing we know we are here on Earth to do.

Ever since I was a little kid, I've had this underlying sense that there was something specific in life I was supposed to be doing. Many people I meet tell me they feel the same way, but they're not exactly sure what it is. Often, they have something they love to do but don't have much time or energy to devote to it because they're too busy making a living.

Many of us have a long standing belief that being financially successful and doing what we love is somehow incompatible. We see others who have a "gift" or talent that they love and who are able to make money from it, but these individuals seem like the exception rather than the rule. I'm not only convinced that we can make a living with our unique expression; it is in fact a key component to our success. When we start to look at our choice of work in terms of how we are spending our most precious commodities, namely our energy and attention, we will likely realize that we can't afford to be working in a job that doesn't energize and fill us with a sense of purpose.

Some people take jobs they don't like but pay well so that they can have their evenings and weekends free to do the things they love, but they'll probably end up spending more time working than enjoying their free time. If we're spending a great deal of time in a job that drains our energy to such an extent that we have only a little bit left when we're actually able to relax and enjoy ourselves, we could say that energetically speaking, we're living beyond our means. We will most likely find ourselves needing to get energy from the people around us, particularly those we love, and have very little to give back in return. On the level that really counts, the math doesn't add up.

Many people justify their lifestyle from a financial standpoint and tell themselves they'll reap its rewards when they retire, but I'd argue that the fantasy of sitting poolside and playing golf in the twilight of our lives may not be as fulfilling as we think. I work with many retirees, and it's rare that I see someone who really enjoys a life of nothing but leisure. Many retirees actually become depressed without a sense of purpose and often return to the workforce, not out of financial need, but in search of greater meaning, and often discover a whole new sense of purpose as they spend more of their time doing what they truly love to do.

As Richard Branson, the founder of Virgin Group and one of the most successful out-of-the-box businessmen of our time said in an interview with *Money* magazine, "If you're into kite-surfing and you want to become an entrepreneur, do it with kite-surfing. . . . If you can indulge in your passion, life will be far more interesting than if you're just working. You'll work harder at it, and you'll know more about it." Branson describes how his first business venture came out of a desire to be the editor of a magazine. At age sixteen, he felt so passionately about communicating to other students that he decided to start a magazine of his own, and he became a businessman by accident because he wanted to make sure his magazine would survive. "Most businesses fail," he says, "so if you're going to succeed, it has to be about more than making money."[3]

Owning our unique expression has to do with the area of life that we spend most of our time: our work. It's not just about making money; it's also about earning energy. I like the financial metaphor of earning something, but in a sense it's paradoxical, because the way we earn energy isn't through a process of taking, but actually through a process of giving and expressing. There's no greater source of energy and inspiration than fulfilling our unique purpose and sharing our talents and abilities with the world.

Often, we're willing to give our energy in order to get something in return—whether it be money, attention, or status—but when we find our unique expression, we often discover that simply doing what we love is its own reward. Our unique creative expression is the way that Source expresses itself through us. When we feel a sense of being fueled from within, it's a sign that we're connecting to that deeper Source of energy. We then no longer feel the need to seek energy from other people and the world around us, but instead give our energy to others while simultaneously energizing ourselves.

An essential part of finding our way in the world has to do with taking responsibility for the direction of our lives. It takes focus and commitment to find, develop, and own the particular expression that we each have to contribute to the world. I use the term develop because our creative expression might be something we're already doing, but perhaps only partially or in a way that isn't deeply fulfilling. When I say "own," I mean embrace that expression so fully that it becomes the thing that unites our working, personal, financial, and spiritual lives. Lastly, the idea of contributing relates to a very important distinction, as I think our true uniqueness is found by how we contribute and express ourselves in the world rather than by what is given to us.

In talking to thousands of people around the country, the ones who are successful—and by that I mean fulfilled, happy, and financially stable—seem to be the ones who've found this sense of purpose and expression for themselves. I'm talking about success at a level where we wake up every day excited about the prospect of what we're going to do. The people who are truly happy are those who are so focused on what they're doing that they don't have time to think about whether they're happy or not. Every morning when they wake up, they think they have something to contribute to the world, and if they don't do it they're simply going to burst. Sadly, I meet so many people who are in jobs they hate, or who remember having a sense that there was something they wanted to do but never found it.

Money and Happiness

We live in a culture that tries to convince us that the more money we make the happier we'll be, but as we've already discussed, this is mostly a myth. One relevant study asked participants in four different income brackets how happy they were. For those making less than $20,000 a year, the percentage of people claiming to be "very happy" was 22.2 percent. For those making $20,000–$50,000 a year, the figure rose to 30.2 percent, and for those making $50,000–$90,000 a year, it rose again to 41.9 percent.

Most interestingly, for those making more than $90,000 a year, the percentage of people who were "very happy" barely changed, rising only one percent no matter how high their yearly income was.[4] This study suggests that having our basic material needs met does contribute to happiness, but beyond this, the two are not connected as closely as we might think.

Through my work, I see this idea backed up over and over again. As one of the top producers in my company, I get invited to speak to other financial advisors about how to become more successful. At times, I'm invited to speak to top tier financial advisors, meaning those with at least six-figure incomes, where I find myself sitting in seminar rooms with many people who already make a lot of money and want to make even more. I always tell them that making more money isn't exactly the point, and usually that's not what they're expecting to hear.

A question I often ask is: "How many people remember thinking that if they could make $100,000 a year they'd have everything they ever wanted and needed?" I ask them to think back fifteen or twenty years, to a time when they were a new financial advisor, perhaps making $15,000 a year, and thinking, "If I could just make $100,000 a year I'd be happy, life would be smooth sailing and everything would be perfect." Usually, every person in the room raises their hand and says they remember thinking something like that. My next question is "How many people feel today the way they thought they would feel when they got the $100,000?" It's very rare that I look out and see someone with his or her hand raised.

I hosted a radio show for a number of years called *Beyond Success; Redefining the Meaning of Prosperity,* and on that show I talked to people all over the country who made millions of dollars a year, several of whom were still really miserable. I also talked to many people who were unusually happy and successful, and what nearly all of those people had in common was not the amount of money they made, but that they were each doing what they loved to do. One of the happiest people I know makes about $30,000 a year and is a ski instructor for handicapped children. He gets to ski all year round, and when not skiing for his own pleasure, he finds great joy and purpose teaching handicapped children a new skill.

I also interviewed many authors on the show who had a lot to say about success, happiness, and how to find our true life's purpose. Dan Sullivan, author of *Unique Ability; Creating the Life You Want,* came up with four ways to know when we're in touch with our creative expression: it's an ability other people notice and value; it's something we love doing and want to do it as much as possible; it's energizing for us and others around us; and it's something that we keep getting better at. Author Michael Ray also added some interesting thoughts. He said that when a person finds their creative expression it feels intrinsically meaningful. It feels natural to do; it makes time go by quickly; we look forward to doing it; and it makes us feel good about ourselves.

These observations echo the pioneering work of Dr. Mihaly Csikszentmihalyi, author of the best-selling *Flow: The Psychology of Optimal Experience.* Csikszentmihalyi explored and defined the concept of *flow* as an experience of optimal fulfillment and engagement. He describes his life's work as the effort to study what makes people truly happy. In the opening chapter of his book, he explains:

> In the course of my studies I tried to understand as exactly as possible how people felt when they most enjoyed themselves, and why. My first studies involved a few hundred "experts"—artists, athletes, musicians, chess masters and surgeons—in other words, people who seemed to spend their time in precisely those activities they preferred. From their accounts of what it felt like to do what they were doing, I developed a theory of optimal experience based on the concept of *flow*—the state in which people are so involved in an activity that nothing else seems to matter; the experience itself is so enjoyable that people will do it even at great cost, for the sheer sake of doing it.[5]

Csikszentmihalyi was surprised by the similarities he found in people's experiences across a diverse range of fields and activities. He identified some of the key characteristics of the state he calls *flow,* including a feeling of complete immersion in the activity, which echoes Michael Ray's observation that we forget about time in such moments. As we begin to explore our own creative potential, the insights of these thinkers can be helpful in illuminating the path forward.

The Power of Our Intuition

One of the most important steps in finding and owning our unique expression is learning how to more readily access and connect with our intuition. As I've gotten older, I've realized that there seem to be two voices operating inside of me, often giving me very different messages. The first is that of my chattering mind, but the second is a bit of a quieter voice, patiently waiting for me to hear it should I take the time to listen. This voice seems to localize somewhere between my solar plexus and my stomach, or more simply stated, between my heart and my gut. I believe this to be the voice of my intuition.

At first, our intuitive voice often isn't so easy to hear. Most of us weren't taught in school how recognize or listen to it at all, but I believe that it is perhaps where we may find many answers to the problems we have. Our intuition often scares our mind, as its messages can be non-linear and illogical. Yet my sense is that it may be the compass that brings us back into alignment with a deeper intelligence that is much greater than our ego based thinking mechanisms.

There is a very simple yet powerful exercise we teach at our consulting firm to help people better access their intuition. Let's say you're torn between two options, say A and B, and truly don't know what to do. Option A has its pros and cons, but so does option B, making it hard to know how to proceed. Perhaps you've been going back and forth for some time now between the two, seemingly caught in no man's land.

What we would recommend is this. Take a few moments to meditate, calm yourself down, and quiet your mind as much as possible. Then either ask yourself, or have a friend ask you in the most simple and direct way possible, "Is it option A or option B?" You will need to be as aware and honest with yourself as you possibly can in order to hear the answer that comes first—usually in a millisecond, if not sooner. Our intuition usually knows instantly. Our challenge is to be quiet, centered, and aware enough to hear it.

After this millisecond, most intuitive answers are followed by a "but… " containing all sorts of reasons why we shouldn't listen to our gut instinct. Our advice: *don't listen to anything that follows the "but…"* This is just our mind trying to talk us out of what we intuitively know to be true.

Listening to our intuition often takes a great deal of courage, and can involve a dramatic departure from the thinking mechanisms we've been taught to use since the earliest of ages. My sense is that, in time and with practice, learning how to access and follow our intuition may in fact be where we find many, if not most of the solutions to the personal and collective problems we face.

Sometimes answers are not easy to come by, and if this is the case, take your dilemma into your longer meditations and keep asking yourself questions until the right direction becomes clear. If unsure, try and wait until you are. There is no rush. Our mind often tends to move much faster than our intuition wants to go, and so learning to slow down can be an essential part of the process. As overrated as thinking can sometimes be, perhaps silence and stillness are often too underrated.

As one of the world's greatest sages, Lao-tzu, wrote back in the fifth century BC, "Do you have the patience to wait till your mud settles and the water is clear? Can you remain unmoving till the right action arises by itself?"[6] This message of patience is essential.

There is no set recipe for finding our unique creative expression. If we simply sit by and wait for it to miraculously appear, we may find ourselves waiting a long time, but we can use our intuition and the insights of those who have found some degree of self-actualization in their lives to help us discover and develop our creative gifts. We may find that this process takes time, and as we will discuss in the next chapter, it is also something that is always evolving.

CHAPTER 7
Expressing Ourselves

Your life has an inner purpose and an outer purpose … Your inner purpose is to awaken. It is as simple as that. You share that purpose with every other person on the planet—because it is the purpose of humanity. Your inner purpose is an essential part of the purpose of the whole, the universe and its emerging intelligence. Your outer purpose can change over time. It varies greatly from person to person. Finding and living in alignment with the inner purpose is the foundation for fulfilling your outer purpose. It is the basis for true success.

~ ECKHART TOLLE[1]

I began to discover my own unique creative expression when I was selling insurance. This may not sound like a very glamorous pastime, and it probably isn't the first thing that comes to mind when we think about a unique creative expression, but I actually loved that job and found in it the seeds that created the life I'm living today. I now run a successful financial services company and am also a personal coach, seminar leader, public speaker, and author. The story of how I moved from selling insurance to my present situation illustrates how a creative expression can evolve and develop, and how important it is to hang in there and follow the signs.

As mentioned in the last chapter, when I speak about owning our unique expression, I'm not necessarily assuming it's something other than what we're already doing. When I coach people on this pillar, I usually encourage them to start with the job they're in right now. By using the tools and exercises I'll be sharing in this chapter, you can hopefully find out if the seeds of your creative expression are right in front of you already. If they are, I'll show you how you can make some changes to the job you've perhaps been dragging yourself to each day, so that it can hopefully become something you're excited to get out of bed for in the morning. If not, I hope to help you find where your direction might lie and get you started on a new journey.

It's About the Money

Although it's true that the point of this book is about finding greater fulfillment and purpose beyond making money, I think it's important to begin here for three reasons. First, we obviously need money to survive, so our creative expression needs to make us a living. If it doesn't, our attention will most likely be preoccupied on more pressing issues of survival and security, and it will be very difficult to find lasting fulfillment, even if we're doing the thing we love the most.

Second, there probably isn't going to be time for most of us to work **and** pursue our deepest life interests, so our unique expression should be a part of our work. We have to find a way to get paid to do what we love, and it should be enough for us to survive on at the very least. While our creative expression might not make us fantastically rich, it will hopefully fulfill us in ways that no amount of money can. For example, some people devote their lives to helping others in need, and while these callings often don't make a lot of money, they sustain certain people in such a way that they don't feel the need for much more than the basic requirements for living.

The third reason money is so important is because it points to something deeper than our bank account balance. While our creative expression doesn't need to make us wealthy, it needs to provide what money represents to us and satisfy our deepest core values. I will say more about this in a moment.

It's Not Just About the Money

One day, during one of my worst financial periods, I sat down with a piece of paper and wrote down everything I loved and didn't love about my job. What I loved was filled with a long list: I liked the people I worked with, the flexibility of the hours, the fact that I was constantly learning new things, and the freedom. What I didn't like was only one thing: I wasn't making enough money. That was it. I'd look at that piece of paper frequently over the next two years as I was struggling, and knew instinctively that the lack of money wasn't a reason to give up. I never woke up once during that time of being broke and thought, "This isn't what I'm supposed to be doing," or "I don't want to go to work."

If you're going through a difficult time in your professional life, consider trying the same exercise. Draw a line through the center of a piece of paper, and write down everything you love about your job on the left side and everything you don't like about it on the right. If the list on left is longer than the one on right, and especially if the right side just says, "I don't make enough money," hang in there. In the weeks and months to come, stay focused on the left side of that paper and try to expand your energy in those directions.

If the right side of your list is longer than the left, and you find little or nothing at all that you love about your job, then perhaps the seeds of your unique expression will not flower there, and it's time to move on. Yes, even if you make a lot of money at that job!

Understanding Our Values

In talking to thousands of people across the United States, I've found that asking what money means to them is a very effective way to better understand particular value sets, what shapes personalities, and defines destinies. Take a moment and try to answer this question in a single word: "What does money mean to you?"

I mentioned earlier in the book that most people tend to define money in terms like freedom, security, opportunity, or power. These four words are probably the most common answers I hear. Perhaps your answer is different, but it most likely falls into a similar category.

There are many psychologists, personal coaches, and business consultants that study human nature for a living; analyzing our desires, motivations, and values in considerable depth. Their insights can often help us better understand our personality types, and also how our underlying drives can impact relationships and financial success. One of the most insightful approaches

I've come across is the work of Dr. Steven Reiss, a professor of psychology and psychiatry at Ohio State University, and author of the book, *Who Am I? The 16 Basic Desires That Motivate Our Action and Define Our Personalities.*

Dr. Reiss spent five years developing and testing a new theory of human motivation based on the pioneering work of William James. After conducting studies involving more than 6,000 people, he concluded that sixteen basic desires guide nearly all meaningful behavior. Desires for such things as power, independence, honor, idealism, social contact, romance, and even eating form particular combinations in each individual, which then express themselves as personality traits. "These desires are what drive our everyday actions and make us who we are," he writes. "What makes individuals unique is the combination and ranking of these desires."[2]

For the purposes of this book, we don't need to get into the level of detail that includes our physical and social desires, but it is important to understand some of the most fundamental desires that can influence our success. If you're interested in more fully understanding Reiss's sixteen core desires, I highly recommend his books, *Who Am I?* and *The Normal Personality,* but for now, let's take a more general look at the desires, motivations, and values that impact our success.

What word came to mind when I asked what money means to you? Was it freedom, security, opportunity, power, or something similar? Think about those four words. We probably feel like we want more than one of them, perhaps even all four, but one of them most likely pulls at us more strongly. It's essential that our creative expression not conflict with that overriding motive. It needs to satisfy our deepest and often unconscious desires in a healthy and socially acceptable way.

For example, if your passion is writing but you have a strong desire for power, being the editor of a small local newspaper might not fulfill you, but how about being a scriptwriter for big-budget Hollywood movies? If your overriding concern is security and you love working with young people, the tenured life of a college professor may be much more fulfilling to you than that of a sports coach. If freedom is your desire, then focusing on a job that gives you control over your own time, like a computer consultant, author, or public speaker would most likely satisfy you more than a nine-to-five job.

These four desires are by no means the only ones that impact our success, but in my experience they are the most fundamental. Once you are clear about these desires and what they mean to you, take some time to think about some of the other motivations that drive you. Perhaps idealism is a strong motivating force in your life. In that case, you'll likely need to make sure that your creative expression is aligned with a sense of purpose that fulfills your idealistic motives. Maybe you're a naturally curious person who loves to learn. If so, your creative expression might need to offer opportunities for growth and innovation so that you don't find yourself bored or frustrated.

When I first got into the insurance business, I was drawn to it by two overriding desires: to be in control of my own destiny and to make a lot of money, which really added up to one thing: freedom. I had an uncle who was a very successful insurance salesman and I could see that he had a lot of money. He worked three or four days a week and then spent a lot of time with his family and pursuing his hobbies. He seemed really happy, and the sense of freedom and happiness he had pulled me towards a career in insurance early on.

Think about the people in your life—family members, friends, colleagues—who seem to have what you want. Talk to them about what they do and how they got there, and find out what they love most about their jobs. What are the most positive and negative aspects? Perhaps you have a friend who owns his own company and always seems to have a great deal of freedom, flexibility, and time to spend with his family. He may tell you that he loves that freedom, but the downside is the sense of insecurity and worry about whether he can make a profit each year. Then ask yourself, "Could I live that way?" Maybe freedom means that much to you too, but perhaps security is a stronger value, and so you'd never be happy living with that degree of risk and uncertainty.

Asking these kinds of questions can help us get a sense of the hierarchy of our own values and needs. This is an important part of the process of finding and owning our unique creative expression. If we don't take into account our core values and desires we are likely to find ourselves derailed, time and again, without quite knowing why.

Conflicting Values

Have you ever been convinced that you wanted to achieve a certain goal but at the same time realized you're unintentionally sabotaging yourself? It could be because what you think you want to achieve is conflicting with a deeper desire of which you're not fully aware.

For example, you might be someone with very little interest in power. Your current job involves supervising a small group of people, and although you're efficient and good at what you do, you keep making mistakes that prevent you from being promoted. You may unconsciously be derailing your career development to avoid more responsibility and having to manage more people.

Knowing ourselves as best we can is an essential part of engaging with this pillar. Start with the job you're in, and ask yourself whether it satisfies your core desires and values. If it does, then it will hopefully give you confidence that you're already headed in the right direction. If it doesn't, it may not mean you're completely on the wrong track, but you may need to take a new angle. As your unique expression starts to come into focus, keep referring back to this foundational question, "Does my job satisfy my core desires?"

Overcoming Discomfort and Uncertainty

Finding our unique expression can be an uncomfortable process at times. It can be disconcerting and even frightening when we begin to disengage from our mind and the unconscious drives that have been keeping us on a narrow track. When we start listening from a more intuitive place, it may initially be hard to hear amidst the tumult of our chattering mind. It can be challenging, because sometimes that voice doesn't make a lot of logical sense and may not be in step with the way we've been taught to think for most of our lives.

We again need to have patience with the process. It may take some time for our direction to come into focus, and there may be different threads within our current lives that seem entirely disconnected, but are destined to come together in unexpected ways. For this reason, I always encourage people to stay open to all possibilities, take one step at a time, and not draw conclusions too quickly. The process may be unsettling at times, but try your best not to let your chattering mind jump back in the driver's seat when things get too insecure.

I never could have predicted the direction my life has gone. Although I initially got into the insurance business motivated by a desire for money and freedom, there were other desires that were also guiding me; intuitions of what would eventually become my unique expression. For example, while in college I had a sense of wanting to be a teacher, but I didn't want to teach a subject like math or physics. I wanted to teach people how to be happier and more fulfilled, but in the beginning I had no idea exactly what that meant. After I graduated, one of the first companies I worked for had me take part in a profiling program to help understand which customer groups best fit my personality. My profile revealed that working with educators was a good niche for me, which in many ways made sense because that was how I saw myself.

I also had a love of public speaking, but my only real opportunity to be on stage at the time was to offer financial seminars, so I began offering them for free at several college campuses throughout New Jersey. Sometimes, I was giving seminars as often as once a week, but was still in search of something more unique and personal that I could teach. By that time, I'd been meditating for several years, and so I began offering meditation classes in addition to the financial seminars. Those classes gave me a tremendous amount of energy and joy, and I intuitively began to feel that I was on the right path.

If It Makes You Happy

If you're seeking the spark of your unique creative expression, whether within your current job or beyond it, take a tip from spiritual scholar Joseph Campbell and *follow your bliss.* You've probably heard that phrase plenty of times and thought that perhaps it sounds nice, but isn't realistic. Following our bliss can often seem like a harder and riskier route to take. Most of us are more comfortable with what is familiar even if it doesn't bring us the joy we're looking for. We have to believe that if we can make a living doing work we don't enjoy, we can get much more out of life by doing work that we love.

The following thirty-day exercise can hopefully give you a clear sense of that direction. This is a short process that I recommend doing each night, but for it to be effective, we need to commit to it for thirty days so that changes are planted deep into our subconscious. Each night before you go to sleep, take some time to reflect on your day. Scan through it like a video recorder and see if you can pause on the most joyful and happy fifteen to thirty minutes. Write down in your journal what you were doing that led you to being so happy. Were you working on a project at work, teaching others a new skill, or building a house? Was it a quiet moment with your child or a friendly debate with your creative team at work? Try to record all the details of exactly what you were involved in when you felt the best and happiest during your day. The next night, do it again without looking back at what you've written. Simply turn the page and don't look back.

Do this every night for thirty nights, then put the journal away for two weeks and leave it alone. After the two weeks, go back and read what you wrote from beginning to end, and look for connections within the thirty days. Is there a pattern that's easily visible? Was it in moments of creative engagement and teamwork that you were happiest? Was it the thrill of taking risks? Was it every time you were working with children? Once we find that pattern and current of joy, it will hopefully help point us towards what we feel we should be doing every day.

Maximizing Our Time

Once we identify the happiest parts of our day, the next step is to look at ways we can eliminate the things we don't like to do so that we can spend more time doing what we love. As my financial practice began to grow, I could easily see that meeting with clients and offering group seminars were the most joyful parts of my day. I could also see that I spent a lot of time doing things I didn't really like to do, including lots of paperwork, making frequent calls to the home office, and chasing after money that needed to be collected.

At the time, there was an assumption in the insurance industry that one person should do it all. I had to be the person who looked for business, closed the sales, did paperwork, and took care of existing clients. These four different roles were sometimes known as being a "finder, binder, grinder and minder." I knew that I was a really good at being a binder and minder; closing a deal and keeping the business, but I was horrible at finding the clients and doing the paperwork; the finding and grinding.

It then dawned on me that if I created a more efficient system that brought people with different talents to work together, rather than having to do all the work myself, together we could actually have more collective success and increased sales. So I developed a business and marketing plan that created the kind of organization I wanted to work in. It was quite radical in the insurance industry at the time, because it was built around a model in which all four functions were different job titles, and I planned to hire people to do those functions separately.

I then partnered with a large international company that gave me the freedom to build the kind of business I envisioned. From the very first day, I made a commitment to hire people, even if only part-time, who enjoyed doing the tasks that I didn't like to do. I loved going on appointments and spending time with existing clients, but hated cold-calling and doing paperwork, so I hired my sister to work part-time to do paperwork, and two other people to make sales calls.

I reviewed what I was doing every six months, and if I noticed something that I didn't love doing, I'd hire someone else do it. Over time, my business grew from one person to forty-five. I teamed up with people who enjoyed and excelled at things I found tedious and frustrating, and the more I did this, the more successful we all became together. So much so that in 2004, my employees nominated me as one of *Fortune Small Business* magazine's "Best Bosses in America," and I won. I know the reason they felt this way about me was because I honored each of their creative expressions.

I do the very best I can to ensure that everyone who works for me feels valued, and I don't try to put square pegs into round holes. As a business owner, it's important for me to match up a job description with someone who has the particular skills, talents, and personality to meet that job. I want the people who work for me to love what they do. When we do employee reviews, we support people in finding their unique expression, even if it means leaving us to go do something else.

My instinct to follow my bliss quickly proved itself, but there was a little bit of faith involved too. In the beginning, I had to pay someone else to do the things I didn't like doing before I actually had the money to afford it. I had to have faith that by freeing up the time to do more of what I loved to do, the money would quickly come in. Fortunately, I found that it usually didn't take more than a few months to make up the income I was paying somebody else to do a job that I didn't want to do, but the willingness to take the initial risk was critical. One of the things that hold back many entrepreneurs is that they're unwilling to delegate any part of their jobs, and they're also reluctant to spend money they don't yet have. The willingness to take a leap of faith can be a major component of success.

Getting Out of Our Own Way

Over the years, I've met thousands of clients and financial advisors, and I've never met two people who are the same. What makes us each unique is not just what we're born with. I believe it's a combination of personal talents, desires, life experiences, circumstances, and relationships that influence us over time. In order to find our creative expression, we need to be sensitive to these different dimensions.

The notion of "getting out of the way" is not just a coaching technique. For me, the moment when we forget about ourselves altogether is paradoxically the point of self-actualization. Transcending the ego-self is the goal of many spiritual traditions, but many of us who've grown up in secular Western culture have a hard time with this idea because we've spent our whole lives being encouraged to develop, improve, and fulfill our "selves." What I love about the idea of a unique creative expression is that it embraces both self-fulfillment and self-transcendence, and in this way it unifies business and spirituality. Abraham Maslow, an American psychologist considered by many to be the father of Humanistic Psychology, discovered a very similar thing when he was exploring self-actualization. He wrote:

> ...[S]elf-actualization work transcends the self without trying to, and achieves the kind of loss of self-awareness and self-consciousness that the easterners ... keep on trying to attain. [It] is simultaneously a seeking and fulfilling of the self *and* also an achievement of the selflessness which is the ultimate expression of the *real* self. [This work] resolves the dichotomy between selfish and unselfish. Also between inner and outer ... the inner and the outer world fuse and become one and the same.[3]

For me, this is the essence of spirituality; when our inner and outer experiences fuse into one expression. All too often, ideas about spirituality focus on a set of ideas or principles. Yet we usually don't think of a person as spiritual because of what they believe in or what they say, we rather tend to look at how they actually live their life. We seem to instinctively know that when their creative expression leaves the world in a better place, the term spiritual is deserved. To me, this is what spirituality and business are about; following our life's purpose and sharing it in a way that helps others. I recently came across a quote from the great jazz legend John Coltrane, which says:

> My goal is to live the truly religious life, and express it in my music. If you live it, when you play there's no problem because the music is part of the whole thing. To be a musician is really something. It goes very, very deep. My music is the spiritual expression of what I am—my faith, my knowledge, my being.[4]

This quote is a perfect illustration of what owning our unique expression is about—being a force for good in the way that each of us can be. It's about being integrated, whole, and finding ways to spend our time bringing together all the aspects of who we are. It's about expressing ourselves in ways that come from our very Source, and then allowing that expression to flow out freely into the world.

So many people look to the outside world to show them what they think they should be doing, and also hope that it will provide them with the energy to do it. Start right where you are and look within. When we start focusing on what we want to express and contribute, we will discover a source of limitless energy and inspiration. Go as deep into yourself as you can.

We can start right now in the job we're doing, and from there begin the evolutionary process of owning our unique expression. Listen carefully for that intuitive voice and look for the joy that is guiding you towards your personal gifts. When we begin to align ourselves with our unique creative expression, our energy will flow from within and we will see its effect all around us.

~ The Third Pillar ~

Redirecting Our Attention

The empires of the future are
the empires of the mind.
~ *SIR WINSTON CHURCHILL*

CHAPTER 8
Investing in Our Future

Let the future tell the truth and evaluate each one according to his work and accomplishments. The present is theirs; the future, for which I have really worked, is mine.
~ NIKOLA TESLA

I can't tell you how many people I meet who make a sizable income, have a family they love and care for, and yet make no provisions for their future. Surprisingly, the percentage of income saved for retirement goes down as people make more money, not up as we might expect. It almost seems that as we make more money we become more convinced that buying more things will make us happier. If I could boil financial planning down to one sentence, it would go something like this: "If you don't invest anything for retirement, you can guarantee it will be pretty miserable." Like most pieces of good financial advice, that sounds pretty simple, obvious, and sensible, but it can be surprisingly difficult to get people to put into practice.

The third pillar offers us similar advice with regard to our attention, and teaches us to invest our energy in who we want to be in the future. The basic principle is that if we don't direct some of our attention towards our future, when we arrive there we won't be in a proper place to be who we hope to be. If we spend all of our time focused on the past or worrying in the present, don't be surprised if the future doesn't look like we hope it will.

Practicing the third pillar asks for five or ten minutes each night. In my opinion, this is a small price to pay to help create a future destination we've chosen. When we begin to consciously devote our attention to the future, our energy seems to grow exponentially in the present, giving us the fuel to create a future that we desire. It's a bit like earning interest on an investment. Einstein famously said that "compound interest is the eighth natural wonder of the world and the most powerful thing I have ever encountered." This statement is just as relevant when the currency is attention.

When I'm training salespeople, I'll often ask, "What are you going to do differently this year than you did last year?" I usually hear something like, "I'm going to make more money" or "I'm going to see more clients," but when I ask them *again* what they'll do differently, they often don't seem to know what else to say.

A well known definition of insanity is doing the same thing over and over and expecting different results. This also holds true at the most fundamental levels of how we spend our attention and energy. If we're living our lives endlessly caught up on the gerbil wheel of our same old thoughts, it's no wonder our lives don't change—even if we attempt to make changes in our outward circumstances.

Our attention often tends to gravitate towards how we feel in the present moment. If we don't feel good, we of course try to do something about it, but what most of us don't realize is that it's in fact already too late, because from a certain point of view, *the present moment has already happened.* Many spiritual traditions, both Eastern and Western, suggest that the present circumstances of our lives are the sum total result of all our past thoughts, speech, and actions; every choice we've made, both consciously and subconsciously, in every moment leading up to now. Subsequently, the only way to really change the present would be to go back and change the past. This is essentially what is meant by the concept of *karma*, which states in the simplest of terms that *every cause has an effect.*

If we plant a tree with a seed we don't want (the cause), there's not much we can do about it once the tree has grown (the effect). It would be foolish to place an orange seed into the ground and expect an apple tree to grow. Good seeds—meaning positive thoughts, speech, and actions, bear good fruit, while bad seeds—meaning negative thoughts, speech, and actions, create situations we don't want—and that we will likely have little control over when they happen. As an analogy, if we throw a rock into a pond, we cannot stop the ripples that come after it.

Regardless of our current circumstances, we can plant new seeds in the present moment, and if we do that skillfully, create a better future for ourselves. Said another way, the more we use positive thoughts, speech, and actions in the present, the more we can change our future for the better. When we begin to take control of what we pay attention to in the present moment, we will be amazed at how quickly our lives can change. Redirecting our attention is about a change of orientation. It's a shift from the past to the present in order to affect our future.

Our lives can change in the most unexpected of ways when we consciously direct our thoughts towards the future we want to create. We may think we want the future to be different, but if we honestly look at our lives, we often find that we don't do much to change ourselves in the present so that we can begin to create something new. Taking control of our future is the real potential that we have in the present. We can consciously plant new seeds now that in time will become the trees and fruits of our future. The key is to plant seeds we actually want through a more skillful use of our thoughts, words, and actions.

Another book that had a big impact on me many years ago was *Advanced Psycho Cybernetics and Psychofeedback* by Paul Thomas. Not exactly the easiest of titles, but this book was pivotal for me. It likened the human mind to a bio-computer with input and output mechanisms, and suggested that whatever we put in is what we get out. If we put in junk, we'll get junk—but if we put in good programs, we'll get good results. His ideas made a lot of sense to me, and I started the program of creative visualization that he recommended in the book.

The process was very simple. I made a little "movie" in my mind that showed me having everything I envisioned for myself in five years time, and I played that movie in my head every night before I went to sleep for thirty days. I visualized that in five years I'd be out of debt, have my own company in a beautiful office building, and have twenty people working for me. I'd be seeing clients all day, talking to them about life, and helping them to reach their goals and dreams. I envisioned living in a big house on two acres of land with a large expanse of woods behind me, and saw myself driving a nice car.

Within a few years, I did get everything I'd put in my movie, but again, the point of this book to go beyond an "I got everything I ever wanted" story. Even so, it is an important point to discuss, because I believe it shows that this idea works. If we have a clear destination and redirect our attention consistently towards it, we will get there—perhaps even quicker than we might expect. Having a direction is essential.

Some people have asked whether this advice contradicts the first pillar and its focus on stepping out of our thought stream, because now we're talking about using our thoughts to create our future. While connecting to Source is essential in helping to break our mind's grip over us, once we've achieved some degree of freedom, we can then begin to deliberately direct our thoughts within that stream. In essence, the two concepts are different parts of a larger whole. Once we've established some degree of control over our mind, we can then get back into the stream in a rowboat and steer our way towards where we want to go. Many spiritual teachers suggest that if we just let go of our thoughts and learn to be in the present moment everything will take care of itself, but I've not found this to be the case. In the words of the inimitable Yogi Berra, "If you don't know where you're going, you'll wind up somewhere else."

A metaphor I like to use is that of my car and its built-in navigation system. When I drive somewhere for the first time, I enter a destination and the navigation system guides me until I get there. It has a camera beside the rearview mirror that looks out at the road in front and sets off a warning system if I start to change lanes without putting my blinker on. It also has a radar detector so that if I set the cruise control and then get within 150 feet of the car in front of me, I will automatically slow down.

Our cars can now increasingly do many of the things that we can do, but there's at least one crucial difference. We still have to tell it where to go and program the navigation system with a destination. Imagine if we got into our car thinking we wanted to go to the city, but instead entered the address of somewhere we went yesterday, last week, or even years ago. We'd end up driving in circles. In a way, our subconscious is a like a navigation system. We're constantly being given directions by our subconscious mind, but if we haven't plugged in the right address and set a proper destination, we are most likely in for a long ride.

Most of the thoughts we have when we're not in control of our mind are negative. Think about how you view yourself in your mind. Do you mostly think about the things you feel you're lacking; that perhaps you're not pretty, smart, or articulate enough? Do you spend most of your time dwelling on things that hold you back? This is how the mind keeps its grip on us. It has a fear of fulfillment, and as a perfection-seeking organism keeps telling us what's wrong. It thrives on negative dialogue, but the more engaged with life we become the less attention we will end up giving it.

Look at how much of our day is accomplished by unconscious mechanisms. Countless physiological processes continue more or less perfectly without us having to think about them at all. Imagine if we needed to remind ourselves to breathe, tell our kidneys to flush out impurities, or instruct our heart to pump blood 108,000 times a day! Our unconscious biological mechanisms accomplish all of these functions, leaving our consciousness free to take care of all the things we still need to think about.

That's what entering a destination address into our navigation system does. It sets a course. The moment I reprogrammed my inner navigation system, I began moving forward at a very fast pace. Within three years, I was the top salesperson in my company and successful beyond what I imagined possible. All it took was a shift of my attention and the readiness to change.

Moving from Audience Member to Director

The metaphor of a movie also is a good one for understanding the third pillar. Somewhere at the back of every movie theater is a light shining through the film, projecting an image onto the screen. The projector represents our attention. The film contains the thoughts, desires, and dreams that motivate us. The light coming through the projector is the light of Source, and the screen it projects onto is our life.

Using this simple metaphor, we can learn a lot about ourselves. What movie are you playing? Where are you in it? Are you an actor in the film, consciously playing out your chosen life, or are you sitting in the audience shouting helplessly at the screen?

If you're sitting in the audience, you're most likely living in the past. By the time that image hits the screen, it's already been scripted. Most of us relate to our lives this way, feeling that somehow we have no control over where we've ended up. We often feel like audience members watching our lives, victims of circumstances and our own unconscious drives.

The first step towards taking responsibility for our future is to take full responsibility for our past and present. We have to accept that we have created the lives we are living today. Any idea or belief we hold that says someone or something outside of us is responsible for the life we're living today—a bad parent, kids who bullied us at school, the dot com crash, a bad business partner, someone who harmed us, or a terrible tragedy we've experienced—serves no purpose other than to keep us stuck where we are. I'm certainly not discounting the impact of those people or events, and I'm not saying that whatever has happened to us in the past is our "fault." This isn't about assigning blame—it's about reclaiming control of our personal power and freedom. We've all been victims at one time or another, but we can either let that victimhood become our identity or choose to rise above it. As long as we see ourselves as victims, we *dis*-empower ourselves. We don't have to deny our past, but we can take responsibility for our present and future.

The third pillar asks us to simply suspend disbelief for a short period of time each day. We have the power to choose what we pay attention to, and over time, if we create a clear vision of a future we want, we can learn to turn our attention away from a habitual downward spiral of thoughts. It doesn't stop the negative thoughts from arising, but the visualization process redirects our attention towards something else. Directing a movie in our mind gives us something fresh and new to put our attention on.

I can't stress this point enough: if we don't fully accept that we are creating *every* aspect of the lives we're living, and that we are the principal authors of our own destinies, writing our own stories every day, we will remain helpless audience members watching our lives go by. However, if we are willing to accept responsibility for the role we've played, and are currently playing in our lives, we will become actors rather than audience members.

Whatever we are experiencing now is the script we've written up until this point. Our responsibility in the present is to be the best expression of that role as we can be, taking full responsibility for our situations, and not blaming anyone else. Only then can we effectively turn our attention to the present and begin creating the future we want. As we learn to do this, anything and perhaps everything can begin to change—sometimes instantly.

This third pillar can take us from audience member—to actor—to the director of our life. Film directors know that each character is an integral part of the larger story. They have a broader goal; to have an impact on the world through making the best possible films they can. Good directors are fully in control of their creations, but they can only hope their messages are well received over time as they place their attention on the movie they're creating. Their attention is glued to the present moment, which is where they can create their future. We can't change the past, and we can't change the present, but we can live our lives now in a way that helps create the future we want. So let's go get a director's chair and start making our movie.

CHAPTER 9
Success is a Journey, Not a Destination

The secret of achievement is to hold a picture of a successful outcome in mind.
~ HENRY DAVID THOREAU

Visualizing our future is a very simple process. All we need to do is create a five minute movie in our mind of us in the future, being the person we always wanted to be if only we had enough money to start. Imagine that money is no longer an obstacle and anything is possible. Our movie should be of us playing bigger in the world and living our unique creative expression to the fullest.

Let's say, for example, that you're a plumber. Your movie might be about owning your own plumbing business, or perhaps working for a company that you find to be meaningful. If you're a teacher, perhaps you want to be a "teacher of the year," creating educational programs yourself rather than teaching other people's ideas.

No matter how successful we already are, there is always a higher level that we can envision. Bill Gates is one of the most successful people in the world, but his goal now is to put a computer in the hands of every child. Bono, the lead singer of U2, isn't just a part of one of the most famous rock bands in the world, but also works to help end poverty in Africa.

The most important thing is that we do what we love. It doesn't necessarily mean we have to be an entrepreneur and strike out on our own. There are plenty of people who love what they do and work for someone else. In your movie, you might be working for someone with whom you have a great working relationship. This way, you don't have the risk and responsibility of owning your own business, but still get to express what you love doing in a comfortable and happy environment.

Sometimes people ask me, "Can I visualize being married to so-and-so?" or "Can I visualize my estranged father finally speaking to me again?" Harnessing the power of our attention gives us the ability to change our own future but not control other people, so the direct answer to these kinds of questions is no. Of course, we all would like our future to be filled with people we love, and it hopefully will, but for the purposes of this exercise it's important to keep our focus on ourselves. This also helps us avoid a common pitfall. Too often, what tends to happen when we include other people in our movie is that we quickly start focusing on what we think they need to change, rather than on what we need to change ourselves.

Your movie should be a snapshot of a day in the life of you. Try to go from morning to night and make it as sensory as possible, so you can see the house you want to wake up in and smell the air when you walk outside. In *Advanced Psycho Cybernetics and Psychofeedback,* Paul G. Thomas explains why this is important:

> There are two ways that a person is able to use his imagination: *objectively* and *subjectively*. When people use their imaginations objectively, it is as though they were looking at a screen and seeing a moving picture. They can "see" themselves doing something, but they do not really

> feel that they are participating in the action. For example, as I am writing this … I can imagine putting down my pen, pushing the chair back, standing up, walking through the French doors, stepping onto the concrete pathway, walking the ten or twelve feet of concrete past the lemon tree… I imagined that, but I did it objectively. I was completely removed from the experience.
>
> With a little more effort, I could have imagined the same thing subjectively. I could actually have felt and *experienced* the same things I was imagining.[1]

Try to add as much detail to your vision as you can, both objectively and subjectively. What kind of car do you drive to work and what do you do when you get there? Whatever it is, it should be you living your fullest expression and being filled with happiness doing what you love to do.

Other Aspects of Our Movie

It's also important to allow room for our movie to evolve. Don't think of it as some ultimate end goal or the pinnacle of success and perfect happiness. Think of it as a reachable first base. We may find that a whole different path opens up for us that we can't yet foresee. Often, when we imagine something bigger for ourselves, we turn our attention to the obstacles we think will come up and the countless reasons why the process won't work. It is important that we suspend all of our doubts.

I also suggest that people not tie their movie too closely to personal financial gain, because as I understand it, our subconscious can only work on images of what we're expressing or doing in the world. Our movie needs to be a clear visual picture of what we have and what we're expressing. Our subconscious can grasp a million different expressions of us acting in the world in a unique way, such as leading motivational seminars or painting in our own studio, but it can't grasp the concept of a dollar. I've seen people try this time and again, and it doesn't work. Our movie has to literally be about us creating as much joy as possible doing what we love to do, while taking into account that money is no longer an obstacle.

The next step in this process takes just five minutes a night before we go to bed. First, spend a minute or two meditating or deeply relaxing. Once you feel comfortable and settled, simply play your five minute movie in your head, and then go to sleep. We then need to play our movie every night for thirty days, so that it can begin to take hold in our subconscious mind. Repeating this process for thirty days will enable us to delve far enough into our subconscious so that it can begin to take us in the directions we'd like to go.

It's also important to pick a future time frame for our movie to take place, but that we not visualize too far into the future. I generally recommend no longer than three to five years. When I started doing this kind of visualization work myself, I used five years as a marker but manifested what I was looking to create in about three. My guess is that for many of us, the time frames for a process like this may become even shorter in the future due to the increasing speed with which things continue to change.

Things are indeed changing so fast that it's difficult to imagine the kind of world we will be living in just a decade or two from now. It hasn't always been this way, as our great-great-grandparents probably had a better sense of the world their children would be growing up in than we do. Technology is allowing us to see results in our lives more quickly than ever before, and in many ways provides an external metaphor for the rapid changes that also seem to be taking place within us, both individually and collectively.

Think about how many things we take for granted today that didn't exist twenty years ago, things like the Internet, iPods, HD television and in-car navigation systems. The first commercial use of e-mail was in 1988, and today, few of us can imagine our lives without it. Moore's Law, named after Intel cofounder George Moore, suggests that the speed of technology is doubling every year, and that the cost is halving. In keeping with this metaphor, it does seem in many ways as if the gap between our internal desires and our fulfillment of them is narrowing at a rapid pace. A lot of this has to do with what we believe is possible, and how concrete our vision is to make this process work.

Act as If

There's an old saying: "act as if," or "fake it till you make it." Act as if you're already a plumber who has his own business, "the teacher of the year," or a successful financial advisor seeing clients that you love to see. Act as if you are already the person you want to be.

When my financial firm had $100 million in assets, I'd walk around the office saying we were a $500 million firm. I'd visualize the number of employees I wanted to have, the type of clients I wanted to attract, the size, look, and location of the office, and the corporate culture I wanted to create. Once we became a $500 million company, I started to visualize a billion dollar firm, and within about seven years we went from having nothing to advising on a billion dollars in assets.

My son Jake has autism, and I serve on the advisory board to the Autism Center of New Jersey Medical School. We held a fundraiser many years ago, and although I had no fund-raising experience myself, we hosted a black-tie dinner with tickets that included special reserve seating for a concert. In the weeks and months leading up to the event, I spent a good deal of time envisioning what it would look like; the venue, décor, menus, guests, and speakers that we wanted to attend. One of the people we included on our list was the then governor of New Jersey, Richard Cody, because we knew he was going to be in the area that night, and we knew that he and his wife did a lot to support mental health initiatives.

We didn't know if he would show up, but continually envisioned that he would, and about halfway through the evening, we got word from security that he was downstairs and would like to come up and say a few words. All the money raised above our costs went to the charity, and the event itself raised $150,000, but during his speech, Governor Cody said that he would match all funds raised at the evening's event which took us to $300,000. Over the next few years, we went on to raise over a million dollars that went towards helping to care for inner city autistic children.

Going Beyond a Destination

It's important to remember that our movie has to keep evolving and is something that often needs to be re-filmed. One of my best friends worked as a computer programmer in a bank, and one day he told me that he wanted to write a book. I suggested he try making a movie about it and spend the next thirty days imagining as concretely as possible "a day in the life of a published author." I suggested that he take it as far as he could, even to imagine the book cover design. He kept coming up with reasons why it would never work, but I told him that it was critical to not focus on any obstacles while going through this process.

Within six months of our conversation, my friend had published his book and sold his first copy, but six months later he was in a total funk again. When I met up with him for dinner, it became clear that he never continued his movie past the moment that his book was published. He didn't realize that this visualization technique is an ongoing process. Now, with the book already published, I encouraged him to visualize using the book to create lectures and seminars, and to script the next chapter of his story.

Life is a journey, not a fixed destination. Think about working with a personal trainer at a gym. A good trainer won't just have us doing the same exercises forever; they'll encourage us to stick with a certain plan until we get results, and then change our routine. Otherwise we're likely to become bored and our results will plateau. I see this often, even with people who have had a lot of success using this technique. They get what they want, but then hit a downward spiral because they have no idea what to do next. We can't use this visualization technique simply because we think the final scene will give us eternal happiness. In the end, we will most likely find that the creative tension and striving is what brings us the most fulfillment and joy.

When I studied economics in college, I learned about the idea of an "S-curve," which shows how businesses and new ideas emerge and develop in the marketplace. It's called an S-curve because it looks kind of like a letter "S" that has been stretched out horizontally. The basic idea is that there is a long initial process of getting an idea into the marketplace, during which the line is basically flat. Once the idea is accepted by the marketplace there is usually a five to seven year period of vertical growth, and the line moves steeply or gradually upward before it levels off and then starts to decline.

This idea seems to apply not only to economics, but also to how we live our lives. That image of the S-curve kept me thinking that if we don't continually evolve our expression in the world, we will eventually hit a period of decline. In business, we're taught to introduce a new S-curve during the declining stage of every prior one. In the same way, the time to start making a new movie is once our old one has become our reality and we are enjoying the fruits of our success.

Although this may logically make sense, we may not feel like doing it at the moment when it's most important that we do. It's easy to envision a movie about what we want to become when we're miserable, but when we've worked hard to get somewhere and are happy, we will probably feel like we just want to relax and forget about the future. If we do, our happiness will most likely be temporary. To return to our financial metaphor, that's like making a half-million dollars a year but not wanting to bother to save and invest for retirement.

Life is an ever-evolving experience, and so is the process of redirecting our attention. With time and practice, creating the future we want can become a learnable skill. The key is to remember that the real seeds of change start from within and then move outward, not the other way around. Let your own experience be your guide. Envision your future as you would like it to be, in as much detail as possible, and see if and how your life begins to change.

~ The Fourth Pillar ~

Expanding Our Awareness

You only have what you give. It is by
spending yourself that you become rich.
~ *ISABELLE ALLENDE*

CHAPTER 10
Giving

The only ones among you who will be really happy are those who will have sought and found how to serve.
~ ALBERT SCHWEITZER

Many of my clients tell me they don't only want to get out of debt, budget their expenses, invest wisely, and save for retirement. Many also want to be able to give, perhaps start a foundation, become a philanthropist, or just make regular donations to a charity of their choice. People I know with strong religious beliefs especially seem to see this objective as an important part of their financial plan. Many religious traditions encourage charitable giving or tithing, and some even recommend that it account for a certain percentage of our income.

The fourth pillar suggests the same thing with regard to our energy and attention. If our attention is the new currency, we need to be giving a percentage of it freely away to others. Again, it may sound simple, but when we try it we may be surprised at just how much of our energy we keep to ourselves, and how little we truly give away without any expectation of return.

The first three pillars are about regaining control of our attention, spending it wisely, and investing it in our future. To continue the metaphor of our attention oriented financial plan, the fourth pillar is about philanthropy. In the conventional sense, philanthropy means "love for humanity, usually demonstrated by giving money to, or doing work for others." When it comes to financial philanthropy, most people who give generously are usually those who already consider themselves wealthy. For most of us, if we can't support our family and pay the daily bills, we most likely won't be writing $10,000 checks to even the most worthy of causes. To some degree this makes sense, but things work very differently when it comes to our attention. Pillar four encourages us to start to give from the very beginning of our transformational journey, even if it seems counterintuitive at times.

A few years ago, I went on a trip to a Land Rover training school in North Carolina. It was quite an experience. The instructor told me, "If you're going downhill on rough terrain and start losing your grip, don't brake." I thought he was kidding. He explained that with this car, we actually had to step on the gas, which is so contrary to everything we're usually taught. The tires would then grab onto the dirt, engage, and provide the stability and grounding we need.

Likewise, giving is often counterintuitive, but it works very much the same way. Just when our instincts tell us to try and hold on to as much as we can get, it is actually in our best interest to do the opposite and find a way to give. This seems like a simple enough idea, but it's one that goes against so many of our deeply imprinted habits. Giving is not an afterthought to success. It is, in my experience, the very foundation. To only be concerned about ourselves is most likely a recipe for eventual unhappiness, while being of service and giving to others is where lasting fulfillment can be found.

The first three pillars are designed to help us develop our unique creative expression. Once we've done that, the fourth pillar suggests that we need to then find a way to utilize that expression in order to help others. This is a scary notion for some people, because so many of us think we need to get as much as we can, lest we be left behind. Yet as the problems we face continue to worsen, it's becoming clear that this isn't a sustainable way for us to live. Unfortunately, so many people still believe it's the only way.

What to Give

When I talk about giving, I'm not necessarily talking about money or even time and effort, although these are also very important things to consider. Remember, the currency of our model is attention, and this pillar uses that same currency. Giving our attention and energy freely to others may be the greatest possible source of energy and fulfillment we can find.

Think for a moment about the times in our lives when we've truly given something to others. Aren't moments like this among the happiest memories we have? Think about how we feel after a day when we've unreservedly given to those we love, whether it's our children, spouse, a friend, or perhaps a complete stranger in need of help. In times like this, we may feel tired physically, but there is often a surprising sense of energy, freedom, and joy that we receive in the process. Compare this to how we feel after a day spent trying to get things for ourselves; perhaps on a shopping trip, a long day making sales calls, or a tough negotiation for a pay raise. After activities like this, we usually feel drained and exhausted, as if we've spent every last drop of our energy in the chase.

I have a client who is a psychiatrist and works with children with learning disabilities and emotional issues. She frequently works twelve-hour days and then often stops to visit one of her nineteen grandchildren. She tells me that she feels more drained trying to make vacation plans for a week away with her husband than she does working these long days giving her attention away.

It's important to remember that all of the four pillars are interconnected, so when we think about giving, please don't think of it as an afterthought. For success to be lasting, giving needs to become an integral part of our unique creative expression. It's a strange paradox, but if we approach the world always looking only for what we can get, chances are we'll get nothing; but if we focus on what we can give and contribute, we can then have anything we want.

If our expression is only aimed at satisfying our own desires, we will not find lasting happiness. If all we are focused on is what we can get from the world, we will find that our cravings are never satisfied. We might seem to get what we want initially, but over the long haul we won't be able to sustain it. Eventually, if we're "lucky" enough to get everything we think will make us happy, we will likely come to realize that it doesn't, which is where the endless loop we've talked about begins to fall apart.

There is another way the loop may fall apart, which in many ways is more difficult. Some people reach a place of utter desperation where they have nothing and then discover a source of fulfillment within. One of the most popular spiritual teachers of our time, Eckhart Tolle, described such a moment in his own life: "Everything felt so alien, so hostile, and so utterly meaningless that it created in me a deep loathing of the world… I could feel that a deep longing for annihilation, for nonexistence, was now becoming much stronger than the instinctive desire to continue to live."[1] This moment of despair, recognizing that "I cannot live with myself any longer," was a catalyst for a profound transformation that eventually led him to a much deeper state of bliss, peace, and joy.

Either of the above scenarios have the power to remove us from the endless cycle and take us off the gerbil wheel. Perhaps you haven't experienced either of them, but nonetheless realize you're caught on the treadmill. The good news is that we don't need to wait. We can step out of the loop right now, and the way to do that is to simply focus on what we can give as opposed to what we can get. Paradoxically, the more energy we put out, the more energy we will have. It's like a boomerang; we throw it out, and then it mysteriously comes back to us. People often ask me why I do so many seminars for free and why I often don't charge for my time. I know that in the currency that really matters to me, I will be more than compensated. Everything comes back when it is freely given.

CHAPTER 11
Beyond Success

No man can sincerely try to help another without helping himself.
~ RALPH WALDO EMERSON

My own understanding of the power of giving came about many years ago, when I was just starting out as a financial advisor. One of the initial appointments I'd have with any new perspective client is what we call in the industry a fact-finding session, where we would meet to gather general information and data; such as a client's date of birth, place of work, income, assets, and so on.

One day, I was getting out of my car and about to walk into a prospect's house to try and sell some term life insurance. I was way behind on my bills, and my mind was going on and on about how much I needed the sale. Desperation poured out of me as I caught my reflection in the car window. I stopped, looked hard at that reflection, and said to myself, "Who would want to buy anything from you? Look at how desperate you look!"

I thought of the successful people in my office and realized that to some extent, they all had a confidence about themselves that I sorely lacked. I decided in that moment that I needed to drop my desperate, needy attitude and walk into this prospect's house with the confidence of someone who didn't want anything. I took one last look at my reflection and saw that I had taken on an air of serenity. That's when I began to realize that I really didn't need anything, and that deep down there was nothing for me to get. I dropped my need to make a sale, and became still and quiet. Soon after, I began to approach more clients this way, putting my attention on them without any expectation for myself. Somewhat to my surprise, my meetings started to transform, and my income began to grow exponentially.

The people I met with also began to open up to me in ways they'd never done before. I literally started to go to my client meetings with absolutely no regard for needing to make money or anything else. I'd simply walk in, shut out the outside world for the hour or two that I was with my client, and put one hundred percent of my attention on them. My fact finding sessions started to become more like therapy sessions. Perspective clients began to express things that they perhaps hadn't spoken about for years, like challenges that they had at home or worries that were eating away at them at work. Many people told me that they felt an intense calm within ten or fifteen minutes of meeting me, simply because I was putting all of my attention on them. Often, we didn't even talk about the stock market, how much life insurance they needed, or what their investments should be. Many of my meetings became a sort of cleansing and bonding session, and the more deeply I gave of my attention, the more rewarding it seemed to be for everyone involved.

I soon began to turn more of my focus and attention towards meditating, finding a deeper sense of peace, and sharing that with other people, and the more I did this the more my income grew. More doors opened up for me as my business steadily expanded, and somewhat to my surprise, I also seemed to have more time to do the things I enjoyed.

A very important thing to understand about giving is that it's not a one-way act of charity. It's an act of mutually beneficial care for the one system we're all part of. I love this quote that is attributed to an aboriginal woman, Lila Watson: "If you are coming to help me, you are wasting your time. But if you are coming because your liberation is bound up with mine, then let us work together." We need to better understand that our liberation, success, fulfillment, and happiness are tied to one another and with the planetary system we share. We're all part of one system, and if we're constantly taking energy from the system without putting anything in, the system will eventually die. The same is true of our individual lives. If we're only concerned with what we personally consume, we will burn out the smaller system that we're a part of, and it too will die.

My frame of mind going into a meeting with another person now is, "How am I needed here?" and the only way I can really figure that out is to become still and put my attention on them. Usually, what's needed then organically reveals itself. Often, I'll go into a business meeting, and when the other person comes in, I can see that they're completely focused on what they want to get. People who think this way usually expect to meet someone on the other side of the table who is also coming in with the same mentality. When this happens, I do my best to come with a mentality of giving, and this often changes the dynamic dramatically.

Breaking the Scarcity Mindset

The idea that giving actually increases energy and taking decreases it is very difficult for many people to grasp. Most of us are caught up in a cultural mindset that says "there's not enough." Despite the fact that numerous studies show that the average standard of living has risen dramatically in the United States over the past fifty years, the percentage of people who consider themselves satisfied with their lives has changed very little, if at all. In his book *The Mind of the Market,* economist Michael Shermer cites a 1994 Princeton Research Associates study that found that less than fifty percent of Americans feel they have enough money to lead satisfactory lives.[1]

"We live with scarcity as an underlying assumption," writes Lynne Twist in *The Soul of Money,* pointing out that this often unconscious mindset of "not enough" and "more is better" plagues the rich as much as the poor.[2] It's in our cultural language: *money doesn't grow on trees; you've got to get your slice of the pie.* Most of the ways we speak about money and resources are based on this conviction of scarcity. If we believe that there isn't enough for everyone, then we believe we have to fight other people for these scarce resources, which is what we see happening in many places throughout the world today. As long as we hold the deep and often unconscious assumption that we've got to get and hold on to as much as possible, we won't be able to focus on giving back and contributing to the health of the system. Perhaps the small area of the world where we live seems to be doing fine, but look at the planet as a whole. The world is burning out, and despite an abundance of resources, large portions of the planet don't have enough of even the most essential needs, such as food and clean water.

It's very difficult to break free of the scarcity mentality. I deal with many people who make six and seven figure incomes a year, many of whom still feel like they don't have enough. There is nothing outside of ourselves that will satisfy the ongoing ache and sense of lack that we all feel inside to varying degrees. We actually feel that ache and emptiness because we are meant to be givers of our energy in service to others rather than takers. Somehow we've flipped the switch and are consumed with taking as much as we can, which is why we all feel like something is always missing.

In an effort to encourage people to change their scarcity-based relationship with money, Lynne Twist writes that "sufficiency resides inside of each of us… In our relationship with money, it is using money in a way that expresses our integrity; using it in a way that *expresses* value rather than determines value."[3]

The same principle applies to the currency of attention. The only way we can ever come to a place where we feel fulfilled and discover the kind of happiness I believe we're all looking for is when we flip the switch. Let's start giving our attention away and using our energy as a means of expressing outward. The more we do this, the happier and more fulfilled I believe we will be.

The most exciting thing about this shift is that we will most likely discover that while taking always reaches a saturation point, giving is infinite and limitless. Think about a time when you desperately wanted some ice cream. There can be a tremendous thrill in initial experience of eating a big bowl, but if we eat too much we quickly find that it leaves us feeling slightly sick. This is what taking too much of anything does to us.

With giving, this doesn't happen. Of course, we all need time to ourselves, and I'm not suggesting that we just constantly give without taking time to care for our own needs, but as long as I budget my time and energy properly, I've never really found myself in a situation where I'm so sick of giving that I just don't want to do it anymore.

Giving in the Business World

Fortunately, we are beginning to see a shift taking place in the business world as corporations begin to understand the value of giving back. This has been especially true in more recent years when it comes to the environment. What the *New York Times* has called "the emerging convergence of for-profit money-making and non-profit mission" is becoming more evident every day, with new books, articles, and advertising campaigns promoting both the virtue and value of sustainable or "green" business.

"I think what people are increasingly looking for, whether in the for-profit or non-profit sector, is how you harness the vitality and promise of capitalism in a way that's more fair to everyone," said Juliana Eades, president of the New Hampshire Community Loan Fund in an article for the *New York Times.*[4] From GE's multibillion-dollar Ecomagination initiative, to Wal-Mart's promotion of earth friendly products, to Unilever's work to help feed children in Asia, the corporate world is beginning to realize that we can't ignore the social and environmental impact of the way we conduct business much longer.

Some people seem to be cynical about the motives of big business for going green, but the point is they are doing it, with more high-profile companies getting on the train every day. As Stonyfield Farms' CEO Gary Hirshberg, author of *Stirring It Up: How to Make Money and Save the World,* puts it, "When these companies go into organics, it's not because they are doing it for moral reasons. They are doing it for financial reasons and therefore, they have a financial stake in its success."[5]

Even if companies are going green for financial reasons, that means this change is consumer driven, which means it is attention driven, which of course takes us back to our currency. Investment bank Goldman Sachs now analyses the environmental, social, and management performance of companies in the same way that it analyzes financial performance. The growing desire among conscience-driven consumers to integrate their spiritual and social values with business and financial success is now also being reflected in trends such as the growth of socially responsible investments, or SRIs.

The surge of nonprofits devoted to "spirit in the workplace" and a growing number of leading business schools, including Harvard, Columbia, and Stanford are incorporating modules on spirituality into their courses and MBA programs. According to Patricia Aburdene, author of the best-selling *Megatrends 2010,* this development has a simple reason behind it: "The personal quest for Spirit has hit critical mass," which she sees as the force that is poised to transform corporate culture: "Spirituality in business, having quietly blossomed for decades, is an established trend that is about to morph into a megatrend."[6]

My point is that all of this starts with us and how we spend our attention and energy. It starts with how we treat each other as human beings and with the understanding that we don't always have to be taking. If we don't start at this most basic level, change will only be superficial. We can give money, time, and effort, and this will make a short-term difference, but it won't change the foundations of the system itself and bring us the kind of happiness I believe we all crave.

Giving Attention

The spiritual author J. Krishnamurti was a great teacher with regard to understanding the power of attention. In his book *This Light in Oneself: True Meditation,* he writes:

> Have you ever given attention to something totally? Are you giving attention to what the speaker is saying? Or are you listening with a comparative mind that has already acquired knowledge and is comparing what is being said to what you already know? Are you interpreting what is being said according to your own knowledge, your own tendency, your own prejudice? That is not attention, is it? If you give complete attention, with your body, with your nerves, with your mind, with your whole being, there is no center from which you are standing, there is only attention. That attention is complete silence ... give your attention to what is being said, so that the very act of listening is a miracle of attention.[7]

The Art of Listening

Have you ever noticed that the words *silent* and *listen* are spelled with the same letters? Perhaps this is no accident, because in many ways they mean the same thing. Have you ever talked to someone and walked away feeling enriched because they were such a good listener, even if they were a complete stranger? This talent is what accounts for some of the best psychologists in the world and also some of the best salespeople. The ability to listen is also the trait most people refer to in a great relationship partner or leader.

Many years ago, I arrived for an appointment with a client of mine. He was a doctor, having a bad day and getting home late from work. He and his wife were frazzled, running around getting ready for me—and their eight year old daughter was bouncing off the walls—happy to have her parents finally home and craving their attention. I remember being acutely aware of how much these people just needed a little peace and quiet more than anything.

I don't even remember what we spoke about. I mostly just listened to them, and within about ten minutes, the daughter fell asleep and the mother leaned back in her chair. The doctor loosened his tie, his breathing calmed, and the frenzied atmosphere in the room relaxed. He turned to me at the end of the appointment and said I must have hypnotized his family. Half joking, he asked me if I could come and do the same thing at 5 p.m. every day!

Have some faith that the Universe has something more important in store than what we can get out of a situation in the moment. If this is true, the only way we're going to see that greater purpose is to become silent, truly listen to the people around us, and see what happens next. Silence doesn't only mean refraining from speaking. It also means quieting the ongoing dialogue in our head so that we can really focus on another person and what they're communicating to us.

The first thing that people often say to this idea is, "If I'm not looking out for myself, I'm going to get walked all over!" Many people assume that if they come from a position that isn't fixed, others will take advantage of them. I've actually found the opposite to be true, because when another person isn't met with resistance, they then begin to back down from their fixed positions, which creates a space for something new to occur. In that space, it often becomes easier to find the right course of action, because there isn't a sense of desperation driving either party to try and get something specific from the situation. It's also easier to protect ourselves and make the right decisions when we're not coming from a needy place. For example, we might go to a meeting, listen to a proposal with our full attention, and then say, "No, I can't do that; it wouldn't be beneficial for both of us." It's not about us walking in and giving away the farm.

Give your attention completely to another person and see what happens. When we're in that space, we'll know exactly what decision to make when it comes to our relationships and our business. Unfortunately, too many of us spend our whole lives waiting to get something from the world so that we can show up as the person we always knew we could be. Deep in our hearts we think there's something missing. When we flip that mindset, we can discover that by becoming a giver rather than a taker, we become agents for change in the world.

The Practice of Listening

Initially, it may be easier to practice the art of listening with strangers. There is such an established energy pattern in long-standing relationships, regardless of whether they are work related or personal. It's often much more challenging to break old patterns and establish new ones with people that are closest to us. For this reason, I suggest that we start to practice the art of listening for brief periods of time where we give our energy freely to someone with whom we don't have a deep relationship or hold any major expectations. For example, see if you can put all of your attention on the person who does your dry cleaning. Take the time to stop for a minute, perhaps ask how their day is going, and really listen to what they have to say.

You'll be amazed at the impact of giving a little attention to a stranger can have. Try it with a cab driver, the barista at your local coffee shop, or the person who delivers your mail. Try it in moments of stress and tension; when the printer hasn't printed your reports on time or the passenger next to you spills a drink on your leg. Then see what happens.

I try to do this every day when I arrive at work. I walk around, say good morning and check in with my employees. I try to pick up on any problems, and if I sense something, see if there is anything I can do to help. The more people are able to open up and flower, the healthier the systems we create are going to be.

Once we've practiced listening with strangers or work colleagues—and experienced for ourselves the powerful effect giving away our attention can have—it would then be a good time to try practicing with our family and close friends. The best time I've found to try this is when I walk through the door after work. Most of us make a conscious or unconscious decision to give our attention and energy at work because we understand the short-term benefits of getting paid. Then, by the time we get home, we're often so burned out and depleted that we walk in the door expecting our spouse to reenergize us. Of course, they are quite likely feeling the same way because they've also been busy working all day and/or taking care of the kids.

I again want to say that it's often much harder with our more personal relationships, because we generally expect so much from them. It might be hard at first, especially if we're running low on energy at the end of the day, but if we come home with the idea that we're going to give as much of our energy and attention to our family as possible, we'll most likely find that they will respond and give us their energy in return. It's very important that somebody be willing to take the first step and break the dynamic of taking. Why not let that person be you?

A View from the Twenty Fifth Mile

One of my favorite days of the year in New York City is the day of the marathon. The energy of the whole city is completely transformed during the hours the marathon takes place, partly because the runners are giving of themselves for a greater cause, but even more so I think because everyone else is so supportive of the runners.

I always go to the same spot to watch the race, in the middle of Central Park, close to the end of the twenty-fifth mile. The runners come past with about one mile to go, and I usually head out there three or four hours into the race. Once, I took my place in the crowd early, when the world-class runners were coming through, but it wasn't nearly as fulfilling. There was nothing they really needed from me, but if you go a couple of hours later, when many of the runners are struggling to various degrees to finish, and sit there cheering them on, I guarantee you'll feel a natural high unlike most others. *Come on! Keep moving! You can do it! You've almost made it!* By unconditionally giving these strangers my energy and encouragement, I feel energized myself. Most of the runners are regular people just like you and me, of every shape and size, and it's an incredible experience to help lift them up that last hill towards the finish line.

I've had a chance to talk many people who have run a marathon, and almost all of them say that the energy they feel coming from the crowds, with everyone clapping, cheering, and rooting for them is overwhelming. What they are left with is not just the relief and euphoria of finishing the race, but the energy they received from the spectators. I think that's why so many people feel that the day of the marathon is one of the best days in New York. It's a testimony to the power and potential that giving unconditionally can have.

CHAPTER 12
Our Legacy

Life is no 'brief candle' to me. It is sort of a splendid torch which I have a hold of for the moment, and I want to make it burn as brightly as possible before handing it over to future generations.
~ GEORGE BERNARD SHAW

Once I finish the process of creating a client's personal financial plan—helping them to save, earn, wisely invest, and share their money philanthropically—there is one final step we take. It's called estate planning, and it's where a client decides what they want to happen with their money after they die. This is the point where a person has to think beyond themselves, how their money can benefit them and ask, "What do I want my legacy to be? How do I want to be remembered? How do I want my impact to be felt when I'm gone by people who love me, and perhaps by others who may not even know who I was?" Similarly, now that we've reached this point in the book and gone through the four-step process of creating a "financial plan for our attention," it's time to turn our focus to the question of our broader legacy.

Before we go on to examine the questions, "What is the legacy of my attention and energy?" and "What imprint will my expression leave on the world?" let's take a moment to reflect on what we've discussed. Through the first pillar, **Connecting to Source**, we learned how to save our attention, become conscious of how we're spending it, and hopefully spend it wisely. The practice of meditation helps us to break the illusory promise that something "out there" will give us the energy we crave, and instead connects us to an infinite Source of energy that we can discover within ourselves.

Through the second pillar, **Owning Our Unique Expression**, we learned how to earn our energy and our money through doing what we love to do. Rather than seeking energy from outside ourselves, we can offer our unique creative expression to the world and find a deep sense of fulfillment in the process. Our creative expression generates energy as we engage in it and can offer us more satisfaction than any object we could possess.

Through the third pillar, **Redirecting Our Attention**, we learned to invest our energy and attention in who we want to be in the future. As we free ourselves from the constant preoccupation of trying to change the past and the present, we can empower ourselves to build the life we truly want.

Through the fourth pillar, **Expanding Our Awareness**, we learned about the power of giving our energy and attention to others. We discovered that we all have tremendous gifts to offer the world in each and every interaction we have.

I now want to take a moment to think about how this process translates into a meaningful legacy. The simplest way I ask clients to think about their legacy is to ask them, "How do you want to be remembered?" This immediately focuses them on tangible actions and contributions. I can't tell you how many times I've heard stories about someone who died wealthy but left no will or estate plan. The family will often say, "He used to talk all the time about what he wanted to happen after he died," but the sad truth is that because he never took action, most of that money ends up being taxed or becoming the object of family squabbles. We don't remember people for the money they left sitting in a bank account. We remember them for what they contributed, what they supported, and what they made possible.

When it comes to our new currency, what we will be remembered for is what we give our attention to. Just as we have to make our estate plan while we are still alive, we have to start actively building the legacy of our attention right now. Our legacy of energy and attention is not about what happens after we die. Every action we take and every choice we make with regard to our energy and attention creates ripples, which then generate waves and turn tides in this world. There is a legacy to every moment.

I like the metaphor of a legacy because it encourages people to think completely beyond themselves and any thoughts of getting something in return. It connects people to a much broader sphere of potential impact than their own circle of relationships. I believe the whole human race is one vast interconnected system, closely interrelated to the planetary system that supports life, and that also depends on us to support and sustain it. What is interesting is that two hundred years ago it would have been much harder to describe this notion to people without it seeming abstract, but today, largely due to the Internet, most of us are connected to our global system on a daily basis.

The phrase "World Wide Web" literally conjures up an image to me of a spider web made up of billions of lines connecting all the people on the planet. During our lifetime, this amazing technology has emerged and can be seen as an outward manifestation of the idea that we are all one large system. Spiritual mystics have told us for centuries that we are all one, but now science and technology are starting to confirm this insight. Albert Einstein once wrote:

> A human being is part of a whole, called by us the 'Universe,' a part limited in time and space. He experiences himself, his thoughts and feelings, as something separated from the rest—a kind of optical delusion of his consciousness.[1]

To adapt Einstein's phrase, this book is about helping us widen our circles of attention. Maybe we all feel so alone and out of balance because we don't feel connected to the larger whole. We all share the same doubts and fears, some of us just hide them better than others.

It helps to know that we are not alone. These days, I think more and more people are realizing this fact, and again, the Internet is playing a big part. Just a few years ago, someone with a particular niche interest or unusual problem might have felt isolated, not knowing where to turn or who to talk to, but today there are chat rooms on every conceivable subject where like minds can connect and discover their sameness.

We all need connection as human beings, and the broader our circles of connectedness are, the more purposeful and meaningful our own lives will become. As we widen our circles of attention, we simultaneously become aware of the impact we can have, even if we are just one in seven billion, one tiny node in the infinite web of humankind.

Just as the Internet makes a great analogy for describing the interconnectedness of billions of people, it is also a great example of the potential impact of one ordinary individual. Have you ever heard of Vint Cerf? I certainly hadn't until I happened to read about him in the back pages of *Esquire* magazine. He actually impacts our lives every day, because Cerf is the man that many credit as being the "father of the Internet." He developed the language that computers use to communicate over the Net, technically known as TCP/IP protocols. What I find fascinating about Cerf (who insists that the fact that his name is pronounced "surf" is just an interesting coincidence) is that he comes across as such an unassuming, ordinary man. Most people may not know his name, yet his invention touches the lives of billions of people every day.

As he told *Esquire,* "there was no one 'Ah-ha!' moment"[2] when he saw where his idea would lead, but it rather was a process that unfolded over time. What I like about Cerf's example is that it points to the impact one individual can have and the kind of legacy that can be created within a human lifetime, thanks to the miraculous speed of change. Thinking about the legacy of our energy and attention requires stretching to see our connection to the broadest circle possible, and recognizing the importance of our own actions and choices in relationship to that greater whole. It's not necessarily about trying to take bigger actions to affect more people. It's about bringing the awareness of that larger context into every small action and interaction we have. The most important thing to remember is that if we want to make a real difference, we have to start with ourselves. We will be amazed at how actual sustained change in ourselves can impact our corner of the world, and how the legacy of our attention can keep expanding out into the wider world and forward into the future.

If this book has had an impact on you, I would urge you to be careful about how you share its message with others. Many of us have a tendency to take something new and pass it on to someone else. That's understandable, as it is part of our human nature to share, but this actually has two negative effects. The first is that unless we allow time to truly digest these ideas and practice them for ourselves, we let ourselves off the hook by passing them on too quickly. It's the mind's way of patting us on the back, telling us we've done a good job and that we don't have to practice any more.

Second, no one likes to be told anything unless they've asked for help first. Too often, someone I've coached will call me and say, "You know, what we talked about yesterday really had an impact on me, but I went home and tried to tell my partner what to do, and they totally didn't get it. Maybe it's because I couldn't explain it well. Perhaps if you could talk to them, you could help." It never helps unless the other person genuinely wants help.

You're the one reading this book, and only you have the power to change yourself. If you practice these techniques you will change, and perhaps people will see that change and then come to you and ask what's going on. We then have two choices. We can pass on a copy of this book, or we can share how our life is changing while being careful not to tell our friends what they need or don't need to do. Just as I've asked you to be gentle with yourself, be even gentler with others. They have their struggles just like us, and if we really care we will listen first and share second. If this book has touched you, the way to share it is not to give other people advice, but to give them the precious currency that this book is all about: attention.

Once we stop trying to fix the people around us and instead focus on listening and widening our circle of awareness, we will discover that we can have an impact on the world in profound and unexpected ways. We will leave a legacy for the future that is not measured in money, but in human energy, which has been generated by freely giving our attention to others. When we give our attention to another human being and that person feels understood, they will stop craving and endlessly taking. When they go home, their energy will then be freed up to be given to others in turn. Freely given attention generates more energy, and energy fuels creativity. That's what our legacy to the world can be, in ways that we may not ever be able to see, but will be felt by people far beyond the sphere of our personal relationships and by generations to come.

This book is part of my legacy, not for its ideas or literary value, but because I've poured my attention and energy into it for the past two years. I hope that through reading and giving it your attention for the hours it has taken you to reach these final pages, you will feel energized, inspired, and begin to take action to transform your own life. If you do, then my legacy will live on through you and all those you give your attention to; not in the form of words and ideas, but as a kind of dynamic creative energy that is the only real happiness I know of. It's a kind of happiness that money can't buy; but attention, when freely given, can and really does have the power to change the world one person at a time.

My deepest personal and spiritual belief is that we do not need to look outside of ourselves for completion, perfection, or fulfillment. We are already complete as we are, and we are blessed with infinite potential. When we connect to Source and have the courage to forge our direction in life from a place of giving rather than taking, the laws of the Universe will mysteriously begin to work in accordance with our wishes and dreams. There is nothing we need to get but rather everything to give. There is an infinite resource of energy within each of us that can be offered up to the world. The world needs us to help transform and sustain it with our infinite energy, passion, and creativity, and it is calling out to all of us. Are you listening?

BEYOND SUCCESS

Redefining the Meaning of Prosperity

To be successful is to be aligned with our unique creative expression in service to the world.

For more information, please visit:

Beyond Success Consulting
www.BeyondSuccessConsulting.com
www.facebook.com/BeyondSuccessConsulting
@GoBeyondSuccess

Gitterman Wealth Management
www.GittermanWealth.com
@JeffGitterman

Author Bios

Jeff Gitterman is an award winning financial advisor and the founder and CEO of Gitterman Wealth Management. He is also the co-founder of Beyond Success, a coaching and consulting company that brings more holistic ideas to the world of business and finance. He has been featured in numerous TV, print, and radio programs, including *Money Magazine, CNN, The Wall Street Journal, Financial Advisor Magazine, New Jersey Business Journal, London Glossy, Affluent Magazine* and *News 12 New Jersey,* among others. In 2004, he was honored by *Fortune Small Business* magazine as "One of Our Nation's Best Bosses." Jeff is the proud father of four children and currently resides in New Jersey. He also serves on the Board of Directors for the Child Health Institute of New Jersey at Rutgers Robert Wood Johnson Medical School and is a member of the Advisory Council of the School of Osteopathic Medicine.

Andrew Appel is the co-founder and Creative Director for Beyond Success Consulting. Prior to this, he spent nearly a decade in the entertainment industry, both as an actor and in production and development for a variety of film and television companies in California and New York. He is a Phi Beta Kappa graduate of the University of Wisconsin-Madison, and has also spent time at Oxford University and USC Graduate Film School.

For more information, please visit:
www.BeyondSuccessConsulting.com
and **www.GittermanWealth.com**

Jeff and Andrew are also Associate Producers of the feature documentary film *Planetary:* **www.PlanetaryCollective.com**

CHAPTER 1

1. Arthur Schopenhauer, *Religion: A Dialogue and Other Essays* (Manchester, NH: Ayer Publishing, 1973), 97.
2. Woody Allen, "Without Feathers," in *The Complete Prose of Woody Allen* (New York: Wings Books, 1992), 63.
3. Søren Kierkegaard, *Eighteen Upbuilding Discourses,* trans. Howard Vincent Hong (Princeton, NJ: Princeton University Press, 1990), 250.
4. Jason Zweig, *Your Money and Your Brain* (New York: Simon & Schuster, 2007), 231.
5. Zweig, *Your Money and Your Brain,* 41.
6. Essentials of Buddhism, Four Noble Truths, www.buddhaweb.org.
7. Sakyong Mipham, *Turning Your Mind into an Ally* (New York: Riverhead Books, 2003), 158.

CHAPTER 2

1. Max Planck, "Das Wesen der Materie" [The Nature of Matter], speech, Florence, Italy, 1944, Archiv zur Geschichte der Max-Planck-Gesellschaft, Abt. Va, Rep. 11 Planck, Nr. 1797.
2. H. A. Simon, "Designing Organizations for an Information-Rich World," in Martin Greenberger, *Computers, Communication, and the Public Interest* (Baltimore, MD: Johns Hopkins Press, 1971).
3. Cited in "Attention Deficit Hyperactivity Disorder," National Institute of Mental Health, www.nimh.nih.gov/health/publications/adhd/complete-publication.shtml

4. John McCain, *Faith of My Fathers* (New York: Harper Perennial, 2000), 206–212.

CHAPTER 3

1. Mihaly Csikszentmihalyi, *Good Business* (New York: Viking, 2003), 188.

CHAPTER 5

1. Quoted in Thomas Egenes and Reddy Kumuda, *Eternal Stories from the Upanishads* (New Delhi: Smriti Books, 2002), 169.
2. Thich Nhat Hanh, *The Miracle of Mindfulness: A Manual on Meditation* (Boston, MA: Beacon Press, 1987), 20.
3. Sakyong Mipham, *Turning Your Mind into an Ally* (New York: Riverhead Books, 2003), 116
4. The Office of Tibet, official agency of His Holiness the Dalai Lama, London, http://www.tibet.com/Buddhism/om-mantra.html.
5. Rick Warren, *The Purpose Driven Life: What on Earth Am I Here For?* (Grand Rapids, MI: Zondervan, 2002), 89.
6. Steven Levine, *A Gradual Awakening* (New York: Anchor Books, 1979), 29–31.
7. Jack Kornfield, "A Mind Like Sky: Wise Attention Open Awareness," *Shambhala Sun* magazine, May 2003.

CHAPTER 6

1. Marcus Aurelius, *Meditations,* trans. Maxwell Staniforth (New York: Penguin Classics, 1964), 126.
2. Figures cited in "The Surprising Profit of Student Loans," *Fortune,* April 16, 2007.

3. Richard Branson, quoted in "Business 2.0: Branson's Next Big Bet," money.cnn.com/magazines/business2/business2_archive/2006/08/01/8382250/.
4. Daniel Kahneman *et al.*, "Would You Be Happier If You Were Richer? A Focusing Illusion," *Science 312,* 1908 (2006).
5. Mihaly Csikszentmihalyi, *Flow: The Psychology of Optimal Experience* (New York: Harper Perennial, 1991), 4.
6. Lao-tzu, *Tao Te Ching,* trans. Stephen Mitchell (New York: Harper Perennial, 1992), ch.15.

CHAPTER 7

1. Eckhart Tolle, *A New Earth* (New York: Penguin, 2008), 258.
2. Steven Reiss, *Who Am I? The 16 Basic Desires That Motivate Our Action and Define Our Personalities* (New York: Tarcher/Putnam, 2000).
3. Abraham Maslow, *The Maslow Business Reader* (New York: Wiley, 2000), v.
4. Paul D. Zimmerman and Ruth Ross, "The New Jazz," *Newsweek,* December 12, 1966.

CHAPTER 9

1. Paul G. Thomas, *Advanced Psycho Cybernetics and Psychofeedback,* (Los Angeles: Paul G. Thomas/Psychofeedback Institute, 1982).

CHAPTER 10

1. Eckhart Tolle, *The Power of Now* (Novato, CA: New World Library, 1999), 1.

CHAPTER 11

1. Michael Schermer, *The Mind of the Market* (New York: Times Books, 2008).
2. Lynne Twist, *The Soul of Money* (New York: W. W. Norton), 45.
3. Twist, *The Soul of Money,* 74.
4. *New York Times,* "Make Money and Save the World," May 6, 2007.
5. Gary Hirshberg, "Why I Wrote My Book," *The Huffington Post,* comments posted on March 10, 2008, http://www.huffingtonpost.com/gary-hirshberg/why-i-wrote-my-book_b_90721.html.
6. All data in this paragraph from Patricia Aburdene, *Megatrends 2010* (Charlottesville, VA: Hampton Roads Publishing, 2005).
7. J. Krishnamurti, *This Light in Oneself: True Meditation* (Boston, MA: Shambhala Publications, 1999), 6.

CHAPTER 12

1. Albert Einstein, Letter to Robert S. Marcus, February 12, 1950, in *Dear Professor Einstein,* Ed. Alice Calaprice (New York: Prometheus Books, 2002) p. 184.
2. Cal Fussman, "What I've Learned: Vint Cerf," *Esquire,* May 2008.